Television in the Antenna Age

Television in the Antenna Age
~ A Concise History ~

David Marc and
Robert J. Thompson

Blackwell
Publishing

BLACKWELL PUBLISHING
350 Main Street, Malden, MA 02148-5020, USA
108 Cowley Road, Oxford OX4 1JF, UK
550 Swanston Street, Carlton, Victoria 3053, Australia

First published 2005 by Blackwell Publishing Ltd

Library of Congress Cataloging-in-Publication Data

Marc, David.
Television in the antenna age : a concise history / David Marc and Robert J.
Thompson.
p. cm.
Includes bibliographical references and index.
ISBN 0–631–21543–3 (alk. paper) — ISBN 0–631–21544–1 (pbk. : alk. paper) 1.
Television broadcasting—United States—History. 2. Television—United States—
History. I. Thompson, Robert J., 1959– II. Title.

PN1992.3.U5M265 2004 2005
384.55′0973—dc22
2004015922

A catalogue record for this title is available from the British Library.

Set in 10/12.5pt Dante
by Graphicraft Limited, Hong Kong
Printed and bound in the United Kingdom
by TJ International Ltd, Padstow, Cornwall

For further information on
Blackwell Publishing, visit our website:
www.blackwellpublishing.com

To America's K-12 teachers

CONTENTS

FOREWORD

Television in the Antenna Age: A Concise History is an apt title, but some might consider it risky. In a world where one must explain what is meant by terms such as "record player" and "LP," is the audience sufficiently familiar with "antenna" to achieve critical marketing mass? David Marc and Robert Thompson have their sights set higher, beyond rooftops, to tell us the real story of how television came to be as it is. With equal measure of incisiveness and impudence, they synthesize the commercial, technological, and cultural benchmarks on the checkered path from telegraph to television to satellite and from *See It Now* to *All in the Family* to *Survivor*.

Among the many histories of broadcasting, this is by far the most entertaining and concise. The authors gleefully unravel the story of modern telecommunications history in all its felicitous, tempestuous, serendipitous, and often ridiculous glory. Like two sets of rabbit ears attuned to cultural and historical trends, they explode the romantic myth that the development of television was driven primarily by enlightened science and aesthetic entrepreneurship. Although they recount the elements of television's Golden Age, affectionately burnishing nuggets of drama, comedy, documentary, and variety, the larger truth is, as they put it, "something less grand." What we get is a mix of intended and unintended consequences, generally flowing more from commerce than art. We are reminded both that news broadcasts were once made of sterner stuff, and that millions of Americans watched mainly because "there was nothing else on."

It's a great story, and Marc and Thompson tell it with comprehensive knowledge, analytic interpretation, and illuminative wit. They remind us why, even when we find television intrusive, deceptive, and even stultifying, we seldom turn it off. Make no mistake, this is a serious book. But the judicious use of sidebars, edifying footnotes, and direct, original quotes from those who were part of television's history keeps the story moving at a pace suitable to, well, television.

Marc and Thompson expound on Marshall McLuhan's insight that "the content of a new medium is a previous medium." And they ingeniously re-imagine modern terms such as software and hardware. For example, early radio programming is reinvented as software: "Depending on software selection, listeners could be re-identified as an audience, a congregation or even a nation"; while the telegraph, crystal sets, and tubes become hardware.

This book is essential for two overriding reasons. First, it helps us to understand how we got to the point where the television tail is wagging the cultural dog. And second, by gaining a more realistic grasp of the chronicles of broadcasting, we may be better prepared for the next transformation.

Laura R. Linder
Associate Professor of Media Arts
Marist College

PREFACE

This concise history of the American commercial television broadcasting industry attempts to cover two parallel sequences of events: a technological period, extending from broadcasting's pre-history in telegraphy to its accommodation with the mass diffusion of cable TV; and a period of popular cultural development, extending from television's immediate artistic pre-history in stage, film, radio, and print journalism to its central positioning in the American entertainment-industrial complex. Otherwise put, we hope to offer the reader a narrative account of how television found its way from the fancy of dreamers, scientists, and bankers to several rooms in most American homes as well as a spectrum of public places ranging from Times Square to the waiting-room of a dental practice.

A surprising number of issues raised by broadcasting in the twentieth century endure as pivotal in discussions of twenty-first-century mass communications. Some examples include the tensions between putative public sovereignty and practical private use of the air as a medium of transmission; the continuing competition between wired and wireless delivery systems; and the conversion of what was once considered the inviolate private space of the home into nothing less than a primary forum of commerce, politics, and other discourses and activities formerly assumed to be "public" in nature.

The book is peppered with previously unpublished comments from television executives, performers, producers, journalists, clergy, documentarians, and other industry operatives. During the late 1990s, I conducted taped conversations with scores of industry operatives to create a record of their impressions and intentions in the making of American television. Some are quoted directly in the book; many more of them influenced its writing. The interviews were done under the auspices of the Center for the Study of Popular Television of the S. I. Newhouse School for Public Communications at Syracuse University, of which Bob Thompson, co-author of this book, is founder and director. Tapes and transcriptions of more than

200 interviews, in their entirety, are now part of the enormous television research collections held by the Syracuse University Library: *http://newhouse.syr.edu/research/ POPTV/contact.html*.

To get these interviews, I traveled an arc of American consciousness stretching from the eastern tip of Long Island to the Santa Monica Pier, with southerly dips along the way through some of America's snazziest retirement communities. Even lacking statistical data, it is safe to say that all the informants, most of whom were retirees, had done quite well for themselves. There was, however, a noticeable diversity in the attitudes they displayed toward the goose that had laid the golden nest eggs.

Among "creative" personnel – producers, writers, entertainers, designers – I met several successful artists and writers who had "used" television to get past the pressures of financial uncertainty, and I also met hacks who had used their television money to convince themselves they were successful artists. The least interesting interview subjects fell somewhere in between.

Newspeople tended to be more wistful. There were more than a few "could-a-beens" and "should-a-beens" muttered about the squandering of the potential that had attracted them to early TV, in most cases from newspaper or radio work. They nonetheless took great personal pride in having reached so many people and in their personal struts upon the stage of history, recounting meetings with the likes of Khrushchev, Elvis, and Cronkite.

Though left in a wide range of emotional conditions by their careers, the network executives seemed to have the most in common in their assessments of the job. They were overwhelmingly sure that they had done a good thing in giving television to America and the world; they were very much aware that not everybody agrees with that appraisal; and they hastened to cite personal philanthropic efforts, and especially efforts on behalf of the fine arts, as a kind of hedge against any apology they imagine that history might one day demand of them.

David Marc
Syracuse, New York
April 24, 2004

ACKNOWLEDGMENTS

Our thanks to George Abbott, head media librarian of the Syracuse University Library, for giving shelter and care to the television history collections; to the Steven H. and Alida Brill Scheuer Foundation for funding many of the oral history interviews that were used in the thinking about this book and writing of it; and to the Lilly Endowment Inc., which provided funding for the Center for the Study of Popular Television's Religious Broadcasters in America oral history project, of which the Pat Robertson interview is a part.

Excerpts from interview transcripts and still photographs captured from videotapes are materials in the Steven H. Scheuer Collection in Television History and the Religious Broadcasters Interview Collection, resources of the Television History Archive, Syracuse University Library, Syracuse, New York.

~ 1 ~
NO SMALL POTATOES

Once upon a time, information was like potatoes. If you had a load to send, it had to be carried. By you or another person. On horseback or foot. By boat or by train. On the leg of a pigeon. On the wings of a dove. It didn't matter: coal, limestone, birthday greetings; love letters, potash, zinc. The news of a political revolution was no different than a ton of bricks or a gross of feathers. Information weighed less than just about anything else, making it an easier burden to physically bear. Yet the consequences of even a single piece of data could be heavy enough to determine the life or death of one person or multitudes.

The War of 1812 provides a good example.[1] Its bloodiest clash, the Battle of New Orleans, resulted in thousands of casualties on both sides. However, that battle took place *after* a peace treaty ending the war had already been signed. How could such a thing happen? It is of course a basic and wise principle of diplomacy to hold peace talks on neutral turf, far from the heat of the battlefield. In this case a treaty ending the war had been negotiated in the Belgian town of Ghent. For the bloodshed to end, however, a tiny bit of information – "The war is over" – lay imprisoned for more than a week in the diplomatic pouch of a passenger on a westbound sailing ship somewhere out in the middle of the Atlantic ocean. Meanwhile, thousands were maimed or killed, families destroyed, homes burned, lives ruined. A quick telephone call, a one-line fax, a radio broadcast shorter than a station break – that's all it would have taken to save all those lives and to prevent all that human misery.

Communication and Transportation: The Divorce

You've probably gotten the message by now, whether from the people whose job it is to be "experts" on TV, or from the schoolteachers who comprise a significant

Logocentrism: words as agents of transformation

The Greek concept of *logos* is difficult to translate into English; it means, literally, the "informing word." *Logocentric* thinking confers a mysterious quality upon words, something beyond their literal meanings. With roots in both Hellenic and Hebraic traditions, Western civilization can be characterized as logocentric. Belief in the power of words to change reality pervades everyday language and therefore everyday life. Here are some examples of how logocentric conceptualization shapes our sense of reality:

- According to the Old Testament, God created the universe not with the aid of physical tools or battalions of workers, but simply by speaking the words, "Let there be light." Words create reality.

- A man and a woman have sex. Their common religion tells them they have sinned and have risked eternal damnation. A few hours later the same two people have sex again. This time their religion tells them they have performed a blessed act. What caused the radical change? They have been "pronounced" husband and wife. In order to pass into this new state of being, each speaks agreement ("I do") to a series of conditions. They do not have to dance, sing, play the drums, or paint pictures. They may exchange rings, but this is considered "symbolic." Words change the nature of behavior and the status of the soul.

- A magician shows the inside of a top hat to an audience to demonstrate that the hat is empty. She places the hat on a table and says "abracadabra." She then reaches into the hat and pulls out a rabbit. What caused an animal to materialize in empty space? We won't get into that now. However, it is implied in the ritual that the word "abracadabra" somehow was the agent of a miraculous physical change. What is implied by the magician's convention of uttering "magic words?" Words transform reality, even in defiance of the laws of science.

- It is against the law to commit murder in Texas. In 2003, the State of Texas purposely killed 24 people. How does the state rationalize what appears to be the breaking of its own laws? Before any such action can take place, the state must "pronounce sentence." With these words, the state declares itself free of its normal obligations to the citizen, and so can kill a citizen. In this case words negate the social contract between individual and society – the very foundation of social life.

segment of their audience, that you live in "the Age of Information." As titles for historical periods go, this is not as impressive as, say, the Golden Age of Greece or the Age of Innocence. To the contrary, "the Age of Information" hits the ear like a song played too often on the radio: repetition has melted it down to intellectual goo. However, if it is possible to recover some significance from this bite-sized and over-chewed little datum, we can probably find it by tracing the origin of the Information Age to a definitive breakthrough in human toolmaking capabilities: the separation of the process of communication from the ordinary problems of transportation.

The inaugural step in isolating the movement of expressed thought from the movement of just about anything else was taken by Samuel F. B. Morse, an American painter, a man spun by The Media of his own times as "the American Leonardo."[2] In 1832 he demonstrated the first reliable long-distance communications device that did not depend on conventional movement through space: the telegraph. By the end of the decade the inventor was granted a US patent.

Morse's telegraph worked something like this: a key struck at Terminal A completes an electromagnetic circuit, causing a piece of metal at Terminal B to become attracted to another piece of metal. As a result, the first piece, rotating on a hinge, strikes the second, which is set beneath it in a stationary position. This produces a tapping sound. Hit the key with a quick finger and the sound comes out short: a dot. Pound the key more deliberately and the sound endures noticeably longer: a dash.[3] As any computer nerd with the social skills necessary for conversation can readily tell you, Morse had articulated a binary system, the basis of modern electronic symbolic intercourse.

Morse had created a mechanism capable of moving electronic impulses through space to a specified point of reception. But without a program to organize those impulses into a language, the telegraph could not function as a communication system. In contemporary terms, the telegraph was hardware in need of software.[4] Morse enabled his new electronic desktop interactive communicator by outfitting it with a custom-made program for translating the electromagnetic sounds it delivered into the letters of the printed English alphabet.[5] With this new language, two people, miles away from each other, could "chat" over a telegraph line by tapping out messages to each other.

Differential improvements of Morse's invention would define the trajectory of communications development throughout the twentieth century: adding voice brought the telephone, subtracting wires yielded radio, adding pictures created television, and so on. However, it was Morse's telegraph that first allowed human consciousness to cross an absolute threshold of competence. The telegraph was not merely a new tool; it marked the opening of a new age of toolmaking. Humanity had extended itself so that it was no longer necessary to be within the range of another person's senses to engage in instantaneous dialogue. A thought could now be extended to another through space without regard for mass or time. Information has been less like potatoes ever since. With the invention of the telegraph, the Sputnik of the cyberworld had been launched.[6]

By the late 1830s, Morse was offering public exhibitions of the telegraph, including a special presentation for President Martin Van Buren and the Cabinet.[7] While politicians and citizens alike found the device impressive, even astounding, most people were generally slow to see profitable uses for it. Some skeptics refused to believe that the telegraph was even possible, dismissing Morse's demonstrations as the tricks of a conman or magician. Others were quick to warn of satanic connections, a position on science and technology that remains popular to this day with a significant segment of the American public. It took Morse and his backers no less than five years of persistent lobbying to finally win a $30,000 appropriation from Congress to build an intercity telegraph-operating system. Even so, both invention and inventor were subject to public ridicule before the measure could be passed.

The first long-distance telegraph line was completed in 1844 connecting the cities of Baltimore and Washington, DC, a distance of about 40 miles. Morse inaugurated service in grand style, answering his critics by giving himself equal billing with the Prime Mover. "What hath God wrought?" he telegraphed across

NO SMALL POTATOES

the not-yet-built Beltway. Two centuries later, we can answer Morse's question: From that moment on, communication ceased to be common freight. We can move information at speeds that divide it from all other commodities.

Is it possible for us today to grasp the impact that the telegraph had on human activity? Try this. Imagine yourself waking up one morning and checking your e-mail, only to see a banner from CNN (or whatever news source your server happens to use) and finding out that the *Star Trek* transporter beam has been invented – for real.[8] Society would be shaken from top to bottom. The remaining airlines might go out of business overnight. The real-estate industry would be revolutionized. You could commute from Tahiti to a job in downtown Chicago. Driving might become a kind of weekend leisure-time activity as it had been for our ancestors. Millions of people would be able to get an extra hour of sleep in the morning, and this could significantly change the character of late-night TV viewing. Prime time might even be extended to midnight (11 p.m. Central). The impact of the telegraph on American life in the nineteenth century was *that* dramatic.

By the mid-1800s telegraph poles were sprouting like the weeds in an organic farmer's garden. One of the immediate casualties of this first great salvo of the communications revolution was the US Pony Express. Launched in 1860 as a crack postal service designed to move mail across the American West by horseback in record times, it was put out of business after only eighteen months upon the completion of the first transcontinental telegraph line in 1861.[9] History itself began to move more quickly.

In 1866, following two failed attempts, a telegraph cable was successfully laid beneath the Atlantic ocean, putting London and New York "online." Although no one knew it, the world was getting wired. The historical trickle of messages was turning into a swelling river of communication that would one day be paved over as the Information Superhighway. This may sound a bit flowery, but elaborate transportation metaphors are still the most common and effective way of describing communication events, even after almost two centuries of separation.

Ironically, the first established communications medium to benefit significantly from the telegraph was print. Today we associate electronic media with the decline of mass print forms, such as daily newspapers and general interest magazines. But initially it was the telegraph that allowed the daily newspaper to establish itself as an effective and reliable source of world, national, and regional information. Even a small-town rag on the western frontier could offer its readers same-day news from Chicago, New York, or Paris via "wire services." One of the earliest of these services was provided by Reuters, a British company. Julius Reuter had actually started his business as a carrier-pigeon service before abandoning birds in favor of electrical telegraphy. Reuters blossomed into one of the premier communications companies in the world, and has remained so in the dot.com era.

Water, Water Everywhere

For all its many practical uses, the telegraph failed to overcome at least one key obstacle to worldwide messaging: the sea. Most of the Earth, of course, is covered by water and for most of history seagoing vessels had been the principal means of conducting international commerce and wielding military power. Ships isolated from contact with the rest of the world had been sailing into oblivion for as long as there had been boats. To be lost at sea is a primal fear of the Western imagination, traceable to the most enduring literary works of ancient civilization. If ship-to-shore radio had existed during the time of Homer, *The Odyssey* wouldn't have been much of a story; an SOS or two and Odysseus is making a bee-line across the wine-dark sea for Ithaca.[10] More than 2,000 years later, the industrial and military needs for a medium of communication that could connect ships with land, and ships with each other, was greater than ever.

With the prospect of big financial rewards, not to mention a chance for the modicum of fame that mention in a textbook might offer, many inventors and wannabees endeavored to build a bridge over space that did not require the stringing of wires. As early as 1872, Mahlon Loomis, a Washington dentist, took out a patent on a device with which he claimed to have sent an instant message to Virginia without the use of telegraph wire. But that same year a great financial crisis, the Panic of 1872, caused research money to dry up, and little was heard from Dr. Loomis after this beyond the screams of his patients. Though many scientists made crucial research contributions, much of the historical credit for the invention of wireless transmission has gone to Guglielmo Marconi.

In 1896, on land owned by his family near Bologna, Italy, Marconi successfully demonstrated a radical communication technology. He transmitted electronic impulses through the air, which were captured by a receiver capable of reprocessing them into what had become the familiar dot-and-dash sound patterns of Morse code. Unlike conventional telegraphy, which moved information in a straight line along a metal circuit, Marconi's "wireless telegraph" transmitted information through airwaves in all directions at once, or *radially*, and so it became known as the radiotelegraph.

In contemporary terms, the telegraph is a *narrowcasting* transmission system; that is, it moves information along a *closed circuit* to a predetermined destination.[11] Radio, by contrast, casts its signal broadly through the air, blanketing a circular zone whose limits are defined only by the power, or wattage, of the transmitter. Thus, in the technical sense, *broadcasting* was born. We can apply these terms to other communication media as well: cable television is a narrowcasting system; a radio station functions as a broadcasting system.

Marconi sought further funding for his project in Italy, but, like Christopher Columbus, who had attempted to sell a radical transportation scheme to Italian

Figure 1.1 Guglielmo Marconi (*right*), inventor of the wireless telegraph, with David Sarnoff of RCA, who applied Marconi's invention to the development of American commercial broadcasting (David Sarnoff Library, Princeton, New Jersey)

Radio: origin of the word

Samuel Morse's telegraph offered users a medium (or "carrier") that was capable of linear transmission; that is, it sent its messages along a wire (or "line"). Marconi's "wireless" telegraph offered two advantages over the Morse system: (1) it could send messages to receivers not connected by wire to the point of transmission; and (2) it replaced linear transmission with *radial* transmission: that is, it transmitted its message in all directions at once, as if it were at the center of a circle. This latter feature led to it being called the *radiotelegraph*. As so often happens in English with practical devices, the word was shortened in common usage to *radio*. In some promotional material issued by inventors and electronics companies, TV is referred to as *radiovision*.

investors some 400 years earlier, Marconi could not find a patron for his communications project in his native land.[12] There was, however, a definite interest, even a hunger, for this kind of technology in Britain. Desire, as always, stimulates faith.

As the nineteenth century came to a close, Britannia, as the song went, ruled the waves. The British empire had reached the pinnacle of Transportation Age power among the nations of the world. It was truly global in a way that no previous temporal power had been. Its list of colonies, dominions, and protectorates numbered in the dozens. To make a journey between just the five largest dominions of the realm – England, South Africa, India, Australia, and Canada – required a complete circumnavigation of the globe. The sun, it was said, never set on the British empire.

British rule, however, was utterly dependent upon the strength and agility of the Royal Navy. Without effective fleets to collect taxes, quell insurrections, keep commercial sea-lanes open, and carry soldiers, missionaries, teachers, and settlers to the remote corners of the world, the empire was merely a way of drawing a map. It was obvious that British power could be significantly enhanced by a communications device that would allow for the instantaneous connection of the empire's far-flung military and commercial fleets to each other, and to the Admiralty back in London.

Marconi's mother was lace-curtain Irish by birth and her family had entrée into appropriate British circles.[13] William Preece, a Royal Mail official who had a personal interest in wireless experimentation, took a particular interest in Marconi's work. Preece's role was crucial in substantiating the credibility of the Italian inventor before the British scientific and financial establishments.

When Marconi moved to London he was only 22 years old. In 1897 he was allowed to start up his own business firm, the Wireless Telegraph and Signal Company, which eventually became known as British Marconi. The pump was primed for research and development to move ahead. In 1899, a wireless message was successfully transmitted 8 miles across the English Channel to France, a modest but symbolically significant demonstration of the new communication technology's conquest of maritime space. Later that year a distress signal from a sinking ship resulted in the rescue of passengers, thus offering a more dramatic demonstration to the world of the practical efficacy of wireless transmission. In 1901, just five years after the first successful experiments, British Marconi sent a radio message across the Atlantic from England to Newfoundland, Canada.

As the company raced toward its goal of making transatlantic wireless communication as common as wired telegraphy, it set up a wholly owned US subsidiary, American Marconi. This subsidiary would eventually pass into American hands and develop into the Radio Corporation of America, the most powerful communications company in the world for most of the twentieth century. But more on that later.

It is worth remembering that, when we speak of these first years of radio's existence, we are referring to a medium whose content had nothing to do with music, shockjocks, football games, or right-wing call-in shows. It may seem hard to believe now, but radio was not intended by its early manufacturers to be an entertainment medium or even a public information medium. It was designed and marketed as a military-industrial tool for interactive business communication in strategic areas where normal telegraph wires were unable to do the job.

Electrical Bananas

The involvement of the United Fruit Company as a pioneering force in radio development offers a good illustration of how radio was used at the turn of the century. In 1904, United Fruit jumped headlong into the business of building radio transmitters, pouring millions of dollars in research and construction capital into its new, fully owned subsidiary, the Tropical Radio Telegraph Company. This was not a wild diversification away from UFC's base in agribusiness, but rather a sound move for a company whose profits were dependent upon the efficient delivery of large quantities of highly perishable fruit.

The company built a string of radio stations covering the route of its product movements from the plantations of Central America to the principal markets on the Atlantic seaboard. This constituted the first broadcasting *network*. With it, ships could be warned of bad weather and ordered to change course, somewhat lessening the danger of the Caribbean basin's notorious rainstorms and hurricanes. Ships could also be redeployed, mid-voyage, to specific markets where their products were bringing the highest prices. As a result, one of the first great achievements of radio was to reduce the number of rotten bananas in the world. United Fruit held several early radio patents and is counted, among such high technology communications companies as General Electric, Westinghouse, and RCA, as a contributor to the research and development (R&D) that paved the way for radio as a mass-communication system.

Here Comes the Judge

When new industries arise, governments are likely to take notice. The first federal law pertaining to radio was the Wireless Ship Act, passed by Congress in 1910. It required all commercial US passenger ships to carry a working radio and a qualified operator. Other safety regulations were added gradually. Freighters were soon required to carry radios as well. Then ships were required to have not one, but two licensed operators aboard. The Radio Act of 1912 set up rules for the operation of land stations. But it also moved government regulation into a new area: the certification of amateur operators, radio's first non-commercial, non-military user-group. Even so, the job of enforcing these regulations remained with the Department of Commerce's Bureau of Navigation. Despite a rising number of individuals who were surfing the uncharted radiowaves for information and entertainment, radio remained primarily a maritime technology.

The benefits of these governmental regulations were graphically illustrated in 1912 when the British ocean liner *Titanic* hit an iceberg and sank in the North Atlantic. Almost a third of the ship's 2,200 passengers were rescued as a direct result of radio SOS signals.[14] The *Titanic* was the largest passenger vessel ever built, and the publicity in the world press surrounding its maiden voyage was already enormous. As a result, the catastrophe left an extraordinary impression upon the public at large. Radio was heroic, a triumph of human ingenuity. The new communications medium had been elevated to the status of a necessity not only in law, but in the hearts and minds of the public. "Necessity," of course, is a standing that the purveyors of all new technologies covet in a consumer-oriented society.[15] If governments wanted to "regulate" the air that carried this modern wonder, it seemed more than reasonable for them to do so.

In retrospect, however, the exercise of early federal authority over radio can be viewed in another light. The seemingly innocent and prudent safety regulations contained in the early Wireless Acts were crucial as important precedents that would affect the future of American free speech. By asserting regulatory power over broadcasting, the federal government, perhaps unwittingly, had claimed fundamental domain over what would later emerge as a crucial medium of human expression and public discourse. Government's ability to impose legal constraints on the use of electronic media remained in force, even though broadcasting evolved into the nation's primary medium of popular culture, something quite aside from rescues at sea.

No such regulatory power had ever been claimed by the American government over the printing press or the movie projector, which was developing at about the same time as radio.[16] In fact, the argument is easily made that a comprehensive rejection of government regulation of public expression was a primary objective of the American Revolution. The struggle to assert government control over the internet is yet another chapter in this history. Advocates of regulation want government to keep both con artists and "objectionable" material out of the medium. Opponents of regulation believe that the threat to free speech posed by regulation is the most objectionable material of all.

Furthermore, in imposing these laws the federal government ventured into new territory that determined its course for much of the twentieth century. The government, in effect, claimed ownership of the air, implicitly asserting its dominion over the air rights stretching up from the dirt beneath a citizen's feet into the stratosphere, the ionosphere, and beyond. Broadcasters must receive a license to use that air, in much that same way that hunters must obtain a license to use public lands.

It is worth noting that the sudden importance of radio waves was not the only reason that the US and governments around the world had become interested in establishing their sovereignty over the air. On the transportation front, another important new technology, the airplane, was taking off. Along with electronic impulse messages, freight (including droppable bombs) was moving through the *ether*, as airspace was then called.

With the Earth's atmosphere emerging as an increasingly important corridor of transportation and communication, governments declared air a tangible commodity and claimed ownership of what had previously been taken for granted as a shared resource belonging to humanity at large. National bureaucracies were established in every country to manage government's hot new property. Little citizen attention was given to any of this in the 1910s. Radio was still a large-scale industrial tool, and, by mid-decade, its advantages as a military apparatus were obvious as well. Only a few visionaries foresaw the possibilities of broadcasting as a means of commercial, political, or aesthetic expression.

Say What?

Signor Marconi was awarded the Nobel Prize for Physics in 1909. His overriding motive for the invention of radio had been to create a tool for the solving of

Figure 1.2 Radio transmitter, circa 1915 (David Sarnoff Library, Princeton, New Jersey)

practical problems, and this he had done to international acclaim. But, as is often the case with industrial processes – from ox-blood cave paintings to computer documents – new left-brain tools create new opportunities for right-brain expression: technology allows industry, and industry invites art, even if the latter invitation is usually through the back door.

The dots and dashes of wired and wireless telegraphy offered little obvious opportunity for artistic expression, though we may surmise, based on the traditions of human behavior, that surely a poem or two, or at least a snappy phrase, was tapped out by a precocious member of the early user-group. However, the next step in wireless development gave birth to radio broadcasting in the form that we know it today: the transmission of natural (or what we now call "analog") sound. If ship-to-shore wireless was a specialized technology on the order of an industrial

NO SMALL POTATOES

mainframe, real sound capability was the breakthrough that made radio a common tabletop appliance.

The large corporations that had developed maritime radio communication – British Marconi, General Electric, and Westinghouse among them – saw analog sound as a mere improvement of the worldwide communication system they were building, and so artistic initiative traveled on its own fuel. The first radio artists were amateurs broadcasting from their own homes. They sang, read poems, lectured, played music, and told jokes and stories over the air to an audience that consisted of each other. They became known as "hams," a lighthearted old theatrical term applied to incorrigible performers.

In addition to being the first true radio broadcasters, many hams liked to engage in an early form of web-browsing known as DXing. This was a kind of compulsive pastime in which users went on air for the purpose of seeing who or what they could discover out there in the radio world. Hams liked to compete with each other over the reach and power of their home-built transmitters and receivers. If a Chicago ham bragged of picking up Des Moines, his neighbor might best him by chatting up Omaha. Ham radio, though a technological relic in the age of the cellphone, is still practiced today as a hobby by a small but devoted user-group.

The story of how the radio learned to speak is a complicated one. Science textbooks rarely take time to parse items of paratextual cultural development, and we will return the favor by avoiding undue scientific detail.[17] Suffice it to say that, as early as 1906, the Canadian inventor Reginald Fessenden had successfully broadcast analog sound – voice and music – from an experimental transmitter in Brant Rock, Massachusetts. His Christmas Eve program of symphonic music astounded wireless operators on ships all over the North Atlantic, and this was a welcome gift, no doubt, for people working the holiday. Another inventor, Dr. Lee DeForest, borrowing heavily from Fessenden's work (too heavily, it is generally thought), set up a transmission tower on the roof of his own home in the Bronx for the purposes of broadcasting to the public.[18] His delivery of the 1916 presidential election results was an indication of the possibilities of radio as a medium of public information.[19]

But the large radio manufacturing corporations were reluctant to enter "show business" or engage in "mass communications" during the early part of the twentieth century. This is well illustrated by the first efforts of the man who would eventually dominate mass-entertainment radio, David Sarnoff. A former telegrapher and now a middle-level official at American Marconi, Sarnoff filed a report to his superiors in 1916, which has since become historically canonized as "the Music Box Memo." In it, he proposed that the company manufacture a line of cheap receiver-only radios to sell to the general public. The appeal of the product would be its ability to receive a channel of broadcast music, offered by a radio manufacturer, at no further cost to the consumer. The memo was not thought worth a response.

Figure 1.3 David Sarnoff sees a future in color TV (David Sarnoff Library, Princeton, New Jersey)

NO SMALL POTATOES

A sociological aside may be appropriate here. Sarnoff was an immigrant from Ukraine who had grown up in the tenement slums of New York's Lower East Side. It was clear to him what the existence of a free source of music might mean to urban families who labored in sweatshops and lived in appliance-less coldwater flats. His bosses, well-to-do Ivy Leaguers, had no such intimate knowledge of the lives, needs, or desires of common people. Nor did they yet see how they might make a bundle off of them in this regard.

Without the benefit of what we would today call "market research," Sarnoff seemed certain that if his parents (and their friends and neighbors and relatives) could have such a "music box" playing in their home, they would make the sacrifice to pay a one-time price for a home radio unit.

Why did top management fail to understand this? For one thing, it was a radical direction in which to take the new electronics industry, and there will always be those more interested in consolidating gains than conquering new worlds. But there were other issues, perhaps more distinctly American, at play. The US, which created itself without a legal blood aristocracy, developed a culture in which one's status is always up for grabs. The country club boys who ran American Marconi saw themselves as businessmen at the cutting edge of a new industrial enterprise, not as purveyors of cheap entertainments to the uneducated masses. That would not become an attractive business for at least another decade.

In 1917 the US sent troops to Europe to fight on the side of Britain and France, which had been at war with Germany since 1914. Entry into the First World War ended a popular tradition of American isolation from European conflicts. The anti-war forces proudly traced their position to the advice of George Washington and Thomas Jefferson. But isolationism was losing its strategic underpinnings in the new technological environment emerging in the twentieth century. The two great oceans that isolationists counted on to "protect" the US from foreign entanglements were beginning to look less great, as space was trivialized by radio communication and airplane transportation.[20]

In the hubbub that surrounded the mobilization of American people and industries to fight a war in Europe, two extraordinary and unprecedented steps were taken by the federal government. The key form of ground transportation in the country, the railroads, was nationalized under direct federal control. At the same time, Washington asserted direct military control over all radio transmission, moving regulatory authority from the Department of Commerce to the Department of the Navy.[21] By executive order of the president, all privately owned radio equipment was seized and sealed under lock and key. The justification in both cases was that these technologies, whatever their other uses, were essential war tools and as such must be under strict government control. In less than twenty years radio had jumped from a laboratory experiment into the most crucial of strategic communications systems, ranking with the railroads as a primary object of national security.

To O. D. Young, Esq. Sheet #13. January 31, 1920.

SALES of "RADIO MUSIC BOX"
For Entertainment Purposes.

For some years past I have had in mind a plan of development which would make radio a "household utility" in the same sense as a piano or phonograph. In 1915 I presented the plan in detail to Mr. Nally, but the circumstances attending our business at that time and since then have not been such as to make practicable serious consideration of this project. However, I feel that the time is now ripe to give renewed consideration to this proposition which is described below:

The Idea is to Bring: Music into the Home by Wireless.

While this has been tried in the past with wires, it has been a failure because wires do not lend themselves to this scheme. With radio, how-ever, it would seem to be entirely feasible. For example – a radio telephone transmitter having a range of say 25 to 50 miles can be installed at a fixed point where instrumental or vocal music or both are produced. The problem of transmitting music has already been solved in principle and therefore all receivers attuned to the trans-mitting wave length should be capable of re-ceiving such music. The receiver can be designed in the form of a simple "Radio Music Box" and arranged for several different wave lengths, which should be changeable with the throwing of a single switch or pressing of a single button.

The "Radio Music Box" can be supplied with amplifying tubes and a loud speaking telephone, all of which can be neatly mounted in the one box. The box can be placed on a table in the parlor or living room, the switch set accordingly and the transmitted music received. There should be no difficulty in receiving music perfectly when transmitted within a radius of 25 to 50 miles. Within such a radius there reside hundreds or thousands of families; and, as all can simultaneously receive from a single transmit-ter, there would be no question or obtaining sufficiently loud signals to make the performance enjoyable. The power of the transmitter can be made 5 KW it necessary to cover even a short radius or 25 to 50 miles thereby giving extra loud signals in the home if desired. The use of head telephones would be obviated by this method. The development of small loop receiving aerials make it possible to devise a small individual antenna to go with each "Radio Music Box". Thus, the antenna problem is likewise solved.

The same principle can be extended to numerous other fields – as for example – receiving lectures at home which can be made perfectly audible; also, events of national importance can be simultaneously announced and received. Baseball scores can be transmitted in the air by the use of one set installed at the Polo Grounds. The same would be true of other cities. This proposition would be especially interesting to farmers and others living in outlying districts removed from cities. By the purchase of a "Radio Music Box" they could enjoy concerts, lectures, music recitals, etc. which may be going on in the nearest city within their radius. While I have indicated a few of the most probable fields of usefulness for such a device, yet there are numberless other fields to which the principle can be extended. Also, the opportunity for selling radio telephone transmit-ters would be increased; for, these would be necessary to the sending part of this project.

In connection with this idea I have had in mind for some time the possibility of connecting up the "Wireless Age" with this plan, thereby making the Wireless Press a profitable venture. What I have in mind is this:

Every purchaser of a "Radio Music Box" would be encouraged to become a subscriber to the "Wireless Age" which would announce in its columns an advance monthly schedule of all lectures, music recitals, etc. to be given in the various cities of the country. With this arrangement, the owner of a "Radio Music Box" can learn from the columns of the "Wire-less Age" what is going on in the air at any given time and throw the "Radio Music Box" switch to the point (wave length) corresponding with the music or lecture desired to be heard.

If this plan is carried out the volume of paid advertising that can be obtained for the "Wireless Age" on the basis of such proposed increased circulation would in itself be a profitable venture. In other words, the "Wireless Age" would perform the same mission as is now being performed by the various motion picture magazines which enjoy so wide a distribution.

The manufacture of the "Radio Music Box" including Antenna, in large quantities, would make possible their sale at a moderate figure of perhaps $75.00 per outfit. The main revenue to be derived will be from the sale of "Radio Music Boxes" which is manufactured in quantities of one hundred thousand or so could yield a handsome profit when sold at the price above mentioned. Secondary sources of revenue would be from the sale of transmitters and from increased advertising and circulation of the "Wireless Age". The Radio Corporation would have to undertake the ar-rangements for music recitals, lectures, etc. which arrangements, I am sure, can be satisfactorily worked out. It is not possible to estimate the total amount of business obtainable with this plan until it has been de-veloped and actually tried out but there are about 15,000,000 families in the United States alone and if only one million or about 7% the total families thought well of the idea it would, at the figure mentioned, mean a gross business of about $75.000,000. which should yield considerable rev-enue.

Aside from the profit to be derived from this proposition the possibilities for propaganda and free advertising of the Radio Cor-poration are tremendous; for, its name would ultimately be brought into the household and wireless would receive national and universal attention.

Figure 1.4 Photostat of David Sarnoff's 1920 memo concerning his 1916 "Music Box Memo" (David Sarnoff Library, Princeton, New Jersey)

Notes

1 The War of 1812 was fought between Britain and the United States, which was composed of a group of former British colonies that had become independent following the revolution of 1776. Washington, DC was invaded and the White House was burned. Despite all the action, there has never been a major feature film or TV mini-series made that concerns the war.

2 This refers to Leonardo da Vinci (1452–1519), an Italian Renaissance intellectual who supposedly was as gifted in the sciences as he was in the arts.

3 In the earliest laboratory models of the telegraph, Morse placed a moving paper tape between the electromagnetically attracted pieces of metal and recorded the "dots and dashes" as physical marks. One of his financial backers, the industrialist Alfred Vail, axed the motorized paper tape system in favor of the sound system. The choice of listening to sound rather than "reading" paper pointed the way to the future.

For more on Samuel Morse, see the *Encarta Encyclopedia* on his life and work: *http://encarta.msn.com/encnet/refpages/RefArticle.aspx?refid=761555922*.

4 At this point in the history of the English language, the term "hardware" still referred to household tools. Software had not yet showed up in the dictionary. But concepts always precede words and Morse had beaten vocabulary to the punch.

5 Morse correlated his code to the Roman alphabet, and specifically to the English language.

6 Sputnik was the first humanly made satellite to orbit the Earth. It carried no devices or passengers. It was launched in 1957 by the former Soviet Union, a compact of more than a dozen nation-states ruled by a central government in Moscow. Members included such modern-day nations as Russia, Ukraine, and Tajikistan. The Soviet Union was dissolved in 1989. Here "Sputnik" is used as a metaphor for the opening of a new technological age.

7 Martin Van Buren (Democrat of New York) became eighth President of the United States in 1837. The term "Cabinet" refers to the group of heads of federal government departments known as "secretaries" (i.e., Secretary of Commerce, Secretary of the Treasury, etc.).

8 As of the writing of this book, no such device has actually been built.

9 During the mid-1980s, the Federal Express (Fedex) company introduced its "Zap Mail" service, in which customers could pay to have e-mail messages sent from Fedex office to Fedex office, with messengers delivering them to people at their homes and offices, thus briefly reviving the "telegraph boy" phenomenon (sexually integrated this time around, of course). However, as home computer sales and mass-market online servers proliferated, the company ended the service in 1990.

10 *The Odyssey* is an epic poem usually credited to an ancient Greek known as Homer (no other name, à la Liberace or Sting). The poem concerns a Greek nobleman and soldier who is trying to find his way home after the end of the Trojan war. Though composed to be recited aloud, it is usually read as a "book" at the few remaining colleges where requirements in classic literature have not been abolished.

11 The term "narrowcasting" is also used sometimes to refer to radio or TV programming which is broadcast in the technological sense, but which is aimed by its commercial sponsors at a particular demographic segment of the possible broadcast audience.

12 The "radical transportation scheme" referred to here is Columbus' plan to sail westward from Europe to reach Asia. After the failure of his attempts to secure funding for his venture in Italy, Columbus gained the backing of the Spanish monarchy. He became the first recorded person of Mediterranean origin to visit the western hemisphere.

13 The phrase "lace-curtain Irish" refers to the wealthy, educated classes of Ireland, a nation otherwise then known for its severe poverty. At this time, Ireland was still under British rule. It would not become an independent republic until after the armed revolution of 1916. Six of Ireland's northern counties remain under British rule.

14 "SOS" is an abbreviation for "save our ship," "save our souls," or some such similar message.

15 Example: Can you live without cable? For decades television viewers did. Previous generations even lived without television.

16 See Robert Sklar, *Movie Made America* (New York: Vintage Books, 1994) for an in-depth treatment of how freedom of expression in film was absorbed into American law and custom.

17 Though we could include it if we wanted to.

18 For an enlightening and entertaining sketch of DeForest's life, see Tom Lewis, *Empire of the Air* (New York: HarperCollins, 1991) or the film adaptation produced by Ken Burns (1994).

19 Woodrow Wilson (D – New Jersey) won a second term by defeating William Howard Taft (R – Ohio) and former US President Theodore Roosevelt (Progressive – New York).

20 The "two great oceans" referred to here are the Atlantic and Pacific.

21 Before the Defense Department was established in the late 1940s, the army and the navy were organized as separate federal departments, each with its own Secretary sitting as a full Cabinet member.

A DOWNSTREAM MEDIUM

One of the great sadnesses of human history is the contrast between dynamic scientific achievement and moral stasis. At no time was this disparity more stark than during the technological spirals of the twentieth century. If humans wielding rocks and clubs were capable of committing unspeakable acts of cruelty upon each other, they proved themselves all the more dangerous in the glow of their more recent intellectual brilliance. The ability to fly, to name one prominent example, had been a noble dream for as long as records of human aspiration had been kept. Once achieved, however, the brute took little time to reassert itself. In 1903, the Wright brothers demonstrated the first heavier-than-air flying machine.[1] By 1914, airplanes were being used to deal death in ways that mock forever the notion that our ancestors were creatures more brutal than ourselves.

So too wireless, having been transformed from a fantastic leap of the imagination into a reliable tool of commerce, found its way to war.[2] New options for the movement of information gave new form to martial impulse. The messages that now flew through the air began proving themselves as powerful as the bombs whose trajectory they shared. For example, German submarine superiority in the North Atlantic should have been able to severely cripple the flow of supplies from the US to Britain. Instead, up-to-the-minute intelligence reports (received by radio) routinely allowed for the issuing of new orders (transmitted by radio). Ships were held at port or ordered to change course mid-voyage as needed. It wasn't just about bananas anymore.

Radio showed signs that it could be an offensive weapon. The sending of phony messages to confuse and deceive enemies is a military tactic nearly as old as war. But here too the speed and efficiency of airborne communication pumped up the stakes and inflated possibilities. Lies moved with the speed of falling bombs. A boom in the production of disinformation began that would span the twentieth century, paving the way to the spam barrages of the internet era. Soon after the

The Zimmermann note

Wireless telegraphy played a political role in the First World War by helping to bring the US into the war. In February 1917, British intelligence intercepted a "private" diplomatic wireless message sent by German Foreign Minister Arthur Zimmermann to his ambassador in Mexico City. In it, Zimmermann proposed a plan to induce Mexico to enter the war on the side of Germany. This would open up a southwestern front that would redirect US military attention away from the North Atlantic. In return for this help, a victorious Germany would cede back to Mexico parts of Arizona, New Mexico, and Texas that the US had taken in the Mexican War of 1848. Zimmermann's "radiotelegram" was front-page news across the country. American public opinion was outraged, especially in the western states, which had been a stronghold of isolationist sentiment.

war, as radio acquired human voice and seeped into the nooks and crannies of domestic space, everyone from carnival pitchmen to fascist dictators would be empowered to distribute elaborate lies on a daily basis to audiences and populations numbering in the tens of millions. Radios, like airplanes and ideologies, would become as indispensable in waging war as guns, knives, and human bodies.

With the aid of these shiny new toys the First World War managed to set new standards for both the quality and quantity of human brutality (though soon enough the bars would be raised on both). With millions dead, physically maimed, and psychologically disabled, the conflict ended when the warring parties signed an armistice on November 11, 1918.[3] The wire services told the newspapers, and the newspapers told the world, that a war to end all wars had been won.

The Show Business

With the threat of foreign invasion thwarted, President Wilson ordered the release of the privately owned radio equipment that the US government had impounded. However, the underlying premise of continuing government regulation of wireless was not seriously questioned. The Department of the Navy, which had taken control of radio during wartime, was not anxious to give up power; bureaucracies rarely are. It was only after extensive Congressional hearings in 1920 that regulation of radiotelegraphy was returned to the Department of Commerce. Had control of wireless communication remained in the hands of the admirals, the transformation of radio into a medium of public entertainment and information might have been delayed by years. Instead it proceeded apace.

American Marconi, severed from its British parent company during the war, was rechristened the Radio Corporation of America (RCA).[4] As we mentioned in chapter 1, in 1916 the company's top management had rejected David Sarnoff's suggestion that it explore the possibilities of radio as a home entertainment business. At first there may have seemed little reason to reconsider that policy. Military air forces and commercial airlines were in startup mode around the world; all needed ground-to-air and air-to-air wireless communication systems. The world shipping industry, recovering from war, remained to be serviced. With a proven product line and an expanding market, RCA might well have been content to remain in the military-industrial business of two-way radio had it not been for an imaginative experiment of one of its rivals.

The Westinghouse Electric Company made the first significant American corporate move toward broadcast entertainment in the summer of 1920 by establishing radio station KDKA, a federally licensed, company-owned transmitting station whose purpose was to broadcast programs expressly meant for as large an audience as it could attract from among the general public.[5] Charging no money to its listeners for these broadcasts (indeed having no way to bill them), Westinghouse sought profits from the manufacture of cheap, receiver-only radio sets which it would supply to mass-market retailers. KDKA was designed as a consumer-tech domestic loss leader, a money-losing venture offered as an incentive for the sale of a money-making product.[6] In contemporary terms, the programs broadcast on KDKA constituted a free software bundle designed to make the company's new line of home desktop "personal" hardware worth buying.

The Westinghouse decision to enter the retail radio market was not a top-down corporate strategy resulting from bravado market research. The idea evolved from the hobby of a middle-level employee. Frank Conrad, a company engineer with no formal experience in the entertainment business, had been a backyard ham radio operator since before the First World War. As a scientist working on naval defense projects, he received permission to keep his transmitter for research and experimentation during the period of government seizure. After the armistice, Conrad resumed ham activities.

His radio station was a mostly do-it-yourself operation, with a single person – himself – looking after both hardware maintenance and software development. Keeping the transmitter in shape was perhaps the easy part for the engineer. Conrad spent a good deal of his effort coming up with talks and lectures, reporting news and sports scores, and presenting live music, much of it played by him and members of his family. Perhaps he made his most memorable contribution to radio broadcasting in the fall of 1919 when he placed a microphone in front of a record-player speaker and transmitted recorded music over the air. This hi-tech labor-saving programming feature proved very popular. Soon Conrad was scheduling programs of recorded music and broadcasting them in specified time slots on a regular basis. As the world's first disk jockey, he even took requests (some of which arrived by US mail).

By 1920 every amateur radio hobbyist within reach of Conrad's transmitter – and every friend and acquaintance of every hobbyist within reach of the signal – knew about the Conrad broadcasts. Horne's, a Pittsburgh department store, was already selling primitive amateur radio sets (assembly required) known as "crystal sets." The store began referring to the Conrad broadcasts in its newspaper advertising as an inducement for the public to buy. News of the phenomenon trickled upstairs to the boardroom. H. P. Davis, a Westinghouse vice-president, suggested that the company cash in by building its own transmitting station and offering local retailers a wholesale line of affordable home radio receivers. Conrad was put in charge of the operation.

The project had modest beginnings, to say the least. A canvas tent was pitched on the roof of a Westinghouse factory in east Pittsburgh to serve as the first corporate radio studio. As the home radios began to sell and the audience/user-group increased, the tent was upgraded to a rooftop wooden shack. Westinghouse set up new stations in Springfield (Massachusetts), Newark (New Jersey), and Chicago. Other companies took notice. The *Detroit News* established a station of its own in 1920, transforming the newspaper publisher into one of the first multi-media communication companies. The nation's dominant newspapers, including the *Chicago Tribune*, the *New York Times*, and the *Washington Post*, would all eventually follow suit.

Back in New York all this activity made David Sarnoff's 1916 Music Box Memo look prophetic – and the executive officers who had ignored it not so prophetic. RCA had blown the opportunity to be there first and now made a determined effort to catch up with its rivals. Sarnoff was pulled up through the ranks to get the company started in the new business of broadcasting to the general public. Soon RCA stations were operating in New York City and Washington, DC. General Electric, the other big manufacturing partner in the radio patents pool, entered the broadcasting business with station WGY, which it built at the company's headquarters in Schenectady, New York.[7]

Thirty stations, most owned by radio set manufacturers and newspapers, were on the air by the end of 1921. Meanwhile all kinds of enterprises were trying to find ways to exploit the opportunities of this new medium, which jumped through locked doors into the homes – and hearts and minds – of the public (also known as "the buying public"). There was a kind of gold rush into radio marketing during the 1920s, much as there would be with internet marketing some seventy years later.

In Philadelphia, Gimbels department store put WIP on the air. In between programs, the store could announce a limited-time sale on a certain item with the hope of mobilizing consumers from all over the region to jump on streetcars and come downtown to the store that very same day. Those same shoppers, as loss-leader theory mandates, having already made the trip, would buy other items, more than compensating Gimbels for losses on the sale item as well as for the expense of operating the radio station. In Los Angeles, as a poetic flourish of history would have it, a car dealership in the San Fernando Valley established southern California's first radio station, KFI. The Ford Motor Company put one on the air in Michigan. These stations offered various types of programs – music, bedtime stories for children, news, stock market reports, sports scores, and so on. Radio was finding form as a conduit of public information and a home entertainment device.

The telephone company or, to be more precise during this period, The Telephone Company, had made significant contributions to radio technology and it too wanted in on the radio bonanza. Today, with dozens of telephone companies engaged in fierce advertising wars for customers, it is perhaps hard to imagine that, for the better part of a century, a single company maintained a government-approved "natural monopoly" over the business. For most of the twentieth century, however, this was pretty much the case. The American Telephone and Telegraph Company (variously known as AT&T, Ma Bell, and The Telephone Company) controlled virtually all long-distance service as well as most local calling. Its research division, Western Electric, conducted experiments in a wide variety of cutting-edge communication media. However, AT&T enjoyed a special advantage that other communications companies did not. Its telephone monopoly served as a guaranteed cash cow that nourished its research and development projects, making Ma Bell a feared competitor in any industry to which she took a shine.

Perhaps it is naive to be surprised, but AT&T management argued, apparently with a straight face, that radio, or the "radiotelephone" as company executives liked to call it, was actually a logical extension of the monopoly the company already held over wired telephone service in the United States. Hoping for a similar concession in radio, AT&T went into the business of owning and operating licensed radio stations.

As part of the terms of its legalized telephone monopoly, however, The Telephone Company could not legally manufacture home radio sets as did radio manufacturers RCA, General Electric, and Westinghouse. Needing to find another way to make money from the new medium, it launched a new business venture at its New York station WEAF, which it called "toll broadcasting." For a fee, WEAF offered to sell blocks of time to buyers, who could use the "radiotelephone" to broadcast as they wished; this of course included making commercial pitches for their products. Once again an analogy to the development of the internet is compelling.

August 28, 1922, though unmarked on calendars and uncelebrated by the closure of banks, schools, or post offices, is nevertheless the day that life, as now lived in the USA, began. It might be called the Founder's Day of post-modern culture. It was the date of the first electronic mass-media commercial. The actual transaction of Broadcast Commercial #1 was exquisite in its modesty and simplicity. In return for the sum of $100, a New York real-estate development company, the Queensboro Corporation, was allowed air time to offer a sales pitch for the apartment complex it was building in Jackson Heights, a New York City neighborhood about 6 miles from midtown Manhattan. Queensboro hoped the avant-garde communication system would be effective in the mass delivery of a very specific piece of information that would significantly enhance the value of its product. A new transit line, which survives today in the New York City subway system as the Number 7 train, had recently been completed through the area, dramatically reducing commuting time to Manhattan work sites. This made Jackson Heights a far more desirable living location for middle-class people than previous public perception had dictated. Sales skyrocketed in response to broadcast advertising. The arts, commerce, domestic life – none would ever be the same.

The home, almost by definition, had previously been a place where one could go to escape the world of commerce; a place where one could relax from the rat race and find, or at least search for, some peace and tranquility among loved ones or in the enjoyment of sheer solitude. The broadcast commercial began a redefinition of the form and function of domestic space. No longer a refuge from the world of buying and selling, the home became, in fact, the *primary* place for commercial advertising (not to mention the primary round-the-clock reception point for whatever horrors, natural or cultural, humanity could manage on a given day).

People willingly, even happily, bought and paid for audio, and later audio-visual, billboards in their living-rooms (and bedrooms and kitchens and bathrooms and dens and so on), inviting the shrill tones of the hard sell, and the saccharine muzak of the soft sell, to become the soundtrack and eventually the setting of their most intimate moments. Music, drama, information, and the other cultural advantages of radio would find new functions as come-ons for retailers. By the last decade of the twentieth century, people would be wearing advertising on their clothing. If internet sales continue to grow, the home may go beyond its function as the principal venue of advertising and in fact become the primary place for commercial transactions as well.

Broadcasting did not initiate this commercial overhaul of living space. It did, however, greatly accelerate a process that had been in motion since the 1700s: the spread of cultural literacy via print. Mass-produced newspapers and magazines, dependent on advertising revenue, became economically feasible as the number of readers steadily increased, and it was these periodicals that established the early beachheads of the consumerist offensive into the home. Broadcasting, however, was the invasion's great Trojan horse. It allowed for the transformation of the home into the place where collective society made its presence most emphatically felt. By the end of the twentieth century it had become common practice to *leave* the home and venture into social space when (or if) the need arose to escape the noise and clamor of the world (to "take a walk" or "go for a drive").[8]

Radical Consumerism Occupies the Middle

Not everybody welcomed this intrusion into the way life had been lived. The principal opposition came from unlikely bedfellows: traditionalist conservatives ("tradcons") and democratic socialists. Understanding the elliptical reasoning leading to this unusual ideological alliance is valuable in understanding contemporary politics, especially the rise of neoconservatism in the twentieth century, which was to a large degree born to refute the traditionalists' abhorrence of unfettered commercial control of culture.

Tradcons, though generally strong supporters of free-market economics, recognized the arts as special, vulnerable activities that required a degree of protection from the predatory operations inherent in commercial intercourse. Moreover, as self-perceived inheritors of traditional (meaning, in America, Euro-Christian) "taste," they were repulsed by the prospect of real-estate agents, used car salesmen, and other tradespeople taking control of cultural programming. Should a soap powder company determine the character of the nation's drama? Should a soft drink company define our music? Should a small appliances manufacturer have editorial control over the news of the world? Radio was fast emerging as a crucial vessel of the English language. The very idea that a bourgeois class of cultural lightweights would be given free rein to call the shots in the divinely inspired pursuits of national culture and taste seemed an abomination to traditionalist conservatives – something not much more desirable than the Bolshevik control of culture which had recently been established in Soviet Russia.[9]

Many American conservatives in the 1920s were more sympathetic to the model of radio development that was being created in Great Britain. The Royal Mail, a state institution, had controlled wired telegraph services in the UK, and that authority had logically been extended to wireless telegraphy. However, as the radio began to talk and play music and put on shows, it became apparent to the British aristocracy that its inherited control of art and culture, as expressed and enforced by church, school, and family training, could easily be bypassed by this new medium. If clergymen, professors, critics, and editors were to remain the "gatekeepers" of British cultural tradition, their authority had to be extended to radio. Yet how could they control cultural access to invisible waves riding through the ether?

Figure 2.1 US President Herbert Hoover (*right*) and RCA Chairman David Sarnoff (David Sarnoff Library, Princeton, New Jersey)

Resistance to commercial broadcasting on the right

In an address to the 1924 Washington Radio Conference, Secretary of Commerce Herbert Hoover warned the nation that allowing commercials to become the major source of revenue in radio could have grave consequences. He speculated that such a system might turn a speech by the President of the United States into "the meat in a sandwich of two patent medicine advertisements."

In 1928 Hoover (1874–1964), a Republican, would be elected President of the United States. When the New York stock market crashed in 1929, precipitating the Great Depression of the 1930s, Hoover refused to take any government action, preferring to allow the free market to correct itself. He became a symbol of early twentieth-century American conservatism. Conservatives today, especially those who describe themselves as "neo-conservatives," are staunch supporters of commercial broadcasting and would likely find Hoover's position on commercial radio puzzling.

As a precaution against loss of cultural dominion, a state-supported enterprise, the British Broadcasting Company (BBC), was created to ensure that the continuity of British culture not be broken by the new medium. Overseen by a board of appropriate royal appointees, the BBC was granted an official monopoly on radio broadcasting. Moreover, a dedicated tax (or license fee) on radio ownership was imposed by the state, and that revenue went directly to the BBC for the production of proper programs, without so much as an annual appeal to Parliament or to listeners or to advertisers for funds.[10] In this way the cultural guardians of the BBC would, at least in theory, be protected from political and commercial interference. This became a model for the building of national radio systems in countries around the world. The BBC effectively kept its authority throughout the radio period, though it lost a good deal of its power during the television era when Prime Minister Margaret Thatcher reformed the British economy to more closely resemble the US model, and a good bit more when satellite cable ended channel scarcity in Britain.

It is much easier to understand left-wing objections to commercial radio. Social democrats saw their worst cultural nightmare coming true in corporate control of radio programming. Here was a resource – the air – which perhaps more than any other belonged to the people who breathed it. Would yet another natural resource of the people be commodified and bought by an elite class of capitalists and then used to squeeze greater profits from the victims of the theft? Apparently so.

Like their right-wing counterparts, political progressives saw a virtue in a state monopoly over radio broadcasting, or in at least maintaining a high degree of state control. Their differences with the tradcons were matters of purpose and content. If the right saw cultural continuity as a pressing goal in the integration of radio into everyday life, the left was more interested in radio as an agent of social change. In radio, social reformers had envisioned (but thus far had not heard) what was potentially the greatest educational and cultural communication tool ever devised for improving the lives of common people.

American businessmen, watching as their handwritten spreadsheets responded to radio advertising campaigns, defined themselves as a virtuous middle between two authoritarian, "un-American" extremes. This was, after all, the United States. No class – whether a bunch of pretentious old elitists (the tradcons) or muddle-headed would-be state bureaucrats (the socialists) – had the right to dictate "proper" culture to the American people. Instead, it was the job of new electronic impresarios to find out what the people wanted – and to give it to them in return for their attention. Let the Invisible Hand play the piano or any other instrument that might gain an audience.[11] Whatever music, drama, and rhetoric finds its way through the marketing jungle could be said to constitute a truly American culture. By the end of the twentieth century it would become difficult to argue with the prescience of this neoconservative vision, though the value of the worldwide popular culture that resulted from its ideological primacy remains a topic that may yet provoke serious debate.

The debate over advertising remained abstract while the sale of home radios by RCA, Westinghouse, and General Electric, and the companies that paid them license fees, boomed. An increasing number of radio listeners were anxious to listen to an increasing number of programs being offered by an increasing number of stations. As the quantity of radio households mushroomed into the tens of millions, however, it became obvious that one day a saturation point would be reached – and then what?

The British system of program finance was actually designed to profit from saturation: new households with radios meant an expansion of the base of annual license-fee payers, which in turn translated into increased funds for program production. David Sarnoff of RCA, taking note, came up with a plan based on the BBC model, but with a distinctively American twist. He proposed that a 2 percent tax on radio sales and subsequent ownership be collected annually by the US government and that, just as in Britain, the revenue of that tax be solely dedicated to program production. However, instead of turning over the revenue to a quasi-public corporation such as the BBC, it would be granted to a private company – his. There was little public support for this plan, and even less enthusiasm among RCA's would-be competitors.

To many Americans, the controversy over the future financing of radio program production pointed to a motive in the founding of the American republic, some 150 years earlier. Should the government become involved in the direct control of a medium of public expression? In their virulent opposition to the Stamp Act and other attempts at British control of print media during the eighteenth century, Americans had invented themselves as such by just saying no. The issue was important enough to become a factor in the collective decision to risk their lives in revolution.

Some differences between publishing and the new medium of broadcasting were recognized and accepted by the public. Because of the nature of broadcasting technology, government was needed as a referee to allocate use of the limited number of available frequencies, and to standardize specifications for transmitting. However, on the issue of free speech, the analogy to print seemed to obtain: governing least is governing best. Neither major political party opposed commercialization, nor is there evidence of a sustained grassroots reaction against it. Business wanted radio as an advertising medium, and that was good enough reason for boom-time 1920s America and its Republican administrations.

Networking

It is doubtful that a radio listener in the early 1920s could have guessed that the hodge-podge of crackling signals emanating from a mixed bag of mixed-use stations operated by a mix of manufacturing companies, retail businesses, and backyard hams would gradually yield the airwaves to an utterly homogenized culture that would systematically consume and digest – or neglect and destroy – any aesthetic variance that came in its path. Furthermore, by standardizing national advertising, radio would become the first great means for building an America whose food, clothing, and shelter were barely distinguishable from one coast to the other. Of all the conquests achieved by communication over traditional geographical obstacles in the twentieth century, this may have been the most impressive.

If the physical compression of space by modern communication systems is traceable to Morse's telegraph, the psychological leveling of culture by speed-of-sound communication might well be marked by RCA's announcement in 1926 of the formation of a new division, the National Broadcasting Company (NBC). Having branched out from two-way radio into mass broadcasting with the establishment of stations in key cities, the company, under the leadership of David Sarnoff, was ready to go beyond the "Music Box" vision of 1916 – and then some.

What is a broadcasting network? A glossary of terms

station any transmitter broadcasting a radio or television signal receivable by standard home equipment

network any group of stations that simultaneously carry the same signal at given times during the broadcast day

o&o a station that is "owned and operated" directly by a network (i.e., the network is the FCC license-holder for that station)

affiliate a station that is not owned by the network, but which has secured the rights to carry the network's programs in its area of service

network feed the signal that is delivered to the stations (both o&o stations and affiliates) constituting the network

clearance any station that is normally part of a given network retains the right to agree or to refuse to carry a program that its network is feeding. Failure to clear a program means that the station chooses to forgo the network feed and to instead originate its own programming during the time period of the program in question

The purpose of the NBC subsidiary was to supply scheduled programs for simultaneous transmission by a network of stations around the country. Since all companies, even RCA, were limited by federal law to owning a limited number of stations, the RCA-owned stations would not be enough to achieve national coverage. In most areas of the country, NBC would seek affiliation with stations owned by other companies. These regional affiliates would retain exclusive rights to carry NBC programs in the radio markets they served.

Network broadcasting would require a new level of technology to link the stations. The Telephone Company, with its system of long-distance telephone lines, provided the solution. Programming would be fed to NBC's network of radio stations via AT&T's "long lines" (special long-distance telephone lines). In return for this profitable hardware contract, The Telephone Company gave up its claim that broadcasting was a "natural" extension of telephone service, agreeing to sell its existing radio stations to RCA and to get out of the business of broadcasting directly to the public. Reconsidered in current terms, AT&T quit the software end of the industry in return for a hardware monopoly over the new process of network broadcasting.

At first RCA operated not one but two national radio networks through the NBC division, the Red Network and the Blue Network. Legend has it that these designations arose from the colors of the push-pins that David Sarnoff used on a map of his national radio empire. The foundation of NBC-Red was the group of stations that RCA had bought from AT&T. It would originate much of its programming from a flagship station, WEAF in New York City. The Red Network went on the air in late 1926 with a total of twenty-two stations carrying its feed. The Blue Network, using RCA's original New York station, WJZ, as its flagship, kicked off programming on New Year's Day of 1927 with live coverage of the Rose Bowl football game from Pasadena. At its start, NBC-Blue had only six stations. By 1941, the last year that NBC operated both networks, there were seventy-four Red stations and ninety-two Blue, with both signals available via high-wattage AM stations in all but the remotest points in North America.[12]

Neither of RCA's major manufacturing competitors, General Electric and Westinghouse, chose to organize competing networks. Instead, both companies affiliated most of their stations with NBC. Ironically, in the 1980s General Electric would end up owning RCA, including, of course, the NBC division. As a property of General Electric, the once mighty RCA would be reduced to the name brand on a line of home entertainment appliances. In 1996, Westinghouse, the other early radio giant, also got into the network broadcasting business by buying NBC's one and only competitor from the 1920s, CBS.

CBS was founded in circumstances quite unlike those that spawned NBC. In 1927, the Columbia Phonograph Broadcasting System (CPBS) took to the air with sixteen stations carrying its programs. Columbia had a different spin on how the possibilities of the new medium might be exploited. A leading record company since the invention of the home phonograph[13] in the late nineteenth century, Columbia hoped to use radio to promote the popularity of its contract recording artists. In fact, according to its original business plan, only the music of Columbia Records artists would be broadcast over the network.

If NBC Radio was an example of a hardware company going into the software business to promote its manufacturing products, CPBS presented the case of a software company going into the hardware business to promote its programming products. The new broadcasting network, however, was at a distinct disadvantage in competing with the two RCA-owned networks. RCA had, quite literally, invented network radio technology, or at least had the patents to prove it. NBC had the most powerful station affiliates, in terms of capitalization and wattage power, solidly lined up in its networks. As if that were not disadvantage enough, CPBS was trapped in the situation of making money for its chief and only competitor in two ways: (1) it had to pay royalties to RCA, which held patents on much of the technology required just to be on the air; and (2) the availability of CPBS helped stimulate the sale of home radios, which meant RCA was made that much the richer in its primary manufacturing business.

In retrospect, CPBS's long-range plan was quite prescient: to dominate popular music by using the new medium as a promotional, star-making apparatus. But could the network last long enough for this experimental plan to be put to the test? Before the end of its first year, it was becoming apparent that the losses of Columbia's radio network might threaten the existence of an otherwise profitable record company. A white knight, however, stepped in to buy the enterprise.

The Congress Cigar Company of Philadelphia, owned by the Paley family, was one of CPBS's chief advertisers. Knowing that an NBC monopoly on network broadcasting would give RCA the power to set rates as high as it chose, and hoping to expand the family's enterprises beyond tobacco, the Paleys stepped in and bought CPBS. William Paley who, like his father, was a cigar maker with no college education, much less a degree in the not-yet-existing academic field of "communications," was sent to New York to see if he could make a go of the family's new high-tech business. Stepping in as CEO, he dropped the "P" ("Phonograph") from the network's name, and presided over the Columbia Broadcasting System's rise to become one of the great communications powerhouses of the world for much of the twentieth century.

Quality Control

Once again, it is appropriate to introduce a transportation metaphor to this discussion of communication history: You are driving in light traffic on the Eisenhower Interstate Highway System. You are hungry. You exit at the suburban rim of a middle-sized metropolitan area. As you drive down the strip toward the city's center, you decide that you would like to eat a hamburger. You see two eating establishments with equally good parking: Ma's Diner and McDonald's. Ma's Diner has a slogan on its roadsign, "World's Greatest Hamburger." McDonald's has a slogan on its roadsign, "Billions and Billions Served." Which do you choose?

While metaphoric exercises are apt to invite romantic choice, there is more than ample evidence that McDonald's is the more likely to get your money. You may already know that McDonald's will not be serving you the "World's Greatest Hamburger," or even if they are, you've sampled the product so many times that you know it won't seem so. Ma, on the other hand, might in fact send you into paroxysms of carnivorous ecstasy. But Ma might also send you into another kind of paroxysm by giving you ptomaine poisoning. If spreadsheets are to be believed, there are numbers in safety.

When we speak of fast food, we usually speak of fast-food chains; when we speak of broadcast entertainment, we usually speak of broadcast networks. When David Sarnoff initiated the network services of the National Broadcasting Company in the late 1920s he assured listeners that they could tune into one of the network's stations anywhere in the country and expect broadcast entertainment to always be a familiar and dependable product. However, the standards he established would at the same time assure a monochromatic quality in culture and rhetoric that would put severe limits on the aesthetic possibilities of the medium. The concept of quality-controlled mass production under development at this same time by Henry Ford on his automobile assembly lines had found application in mass communication.

Notes

1 Wilbur and Orville Wright, two American brothers from Ohio, working without any direct corporate support, are generally acknowledged as the inventors of the airplane. They achieved 12 minutes of engine-propelled flight at Kitty Hawk, North Carolina, in 1903.

2 The war referred to here is the First World War (1914–18), also known as "the Great War" until there was a second. Big winners: Britain, France and, especially, the US, which joined the war in 1917. Big losers: Germany, the Austro-Hungarian empire, and the Ottoman empire (the forerunner of modern-day Turkey).

3 This is the origin of the school holiday now known as "Veterans Day."

4 The corporate history of RCA is a complicated one to say the least. General Electric bought the company from British Marconi, later sold it, and much later bought it back again. However, it was as an independent company (circa 1922–78) that RCA dominated American radio and television development.

5 The claim of being "the first radio station" can arguably be made by station KQW, San Francisco. It was founded in San Jose by Charles "Doc" Herrold at his proprietary College of Engineering and Wireless. As early as 1909, Herrold was manufacturing sets at the college, giving them away free to hotels and other public places, and broadcasting scheduled programs to them. The heritage of current-day KCBS can be traced to the Herrold license. The particular significance of KDKA is that it was a venture launched by Westinghouse, a major corporation holding key patents, and capable of disseminating radio on a mass scale.

6 The term "loss leader" refers to the common retailing practice of a seller offering one or more items at a financial loss in order to gain customers whose other business will more than make up for that loss. In this case the "software" (radio programming) was supplied at a loss to get consumers to buy "hardware" (a radio). The hope was that the profits from selling radios would more than make up for the losses incurred in the running of the radio station.

7 The "patents pool" refers to the agreement of the three big radio manufacturers, General Electric, Westinghouse, and RCA, to share their patents in the field of radio.

8 For these transportation solutions to be successful, however, one must resist the temptation to bring a Walkman along for the stroll, or keep the radio turned off in the car. Even then, it is necessary to contend with the billboards plastered on the streets and on the clothing of any people one may encounter.

9   This refers to the Russian Revolution of 1917, in which a traditional monarchy had been overthrown and replaced by an extreme left-wing faction known as the Bolsheviks.

10   Parliament is Britain's national legislative body, similar to, and older than, the US Congress.

11   Adam Smith (1723–90) was an economist. In *The Wealth of Nations* he described the push of unseen market forces upon people as an "invisible hand."

12   In 1941 NBC was forced by the FCC's "Chain Broadcasting" regulations to sell one of its two networks. The Blue Network passed into other hands and became the American Broadcasting Company (ABC). See chapter 4 for further details.

13   Before the widespread diffusion of home audiotape in the 1960s, followed by the introduction of the compact disk in the 1980s, music was recorded on vinyl discs (and, for a brief time before that, on wax cylinders). The home appliance used to play these discs was known as a phonograph or record player. In the stereo component era, beginning in the late 1950s, the term "turntable" came into use as well. Yet another name for the appliance was the "Victrola," which was originally a brand name used by the Victor Company, which became a subsidiary of RCA.

~ 3 ~
A BURNING BUSH?

"The content of a new medium is a previous medium."
Marshall McLuhan

In 1922 there were fewer than 60,000 households in America with radios in them; that translates to about two sets for every thousand families. In 1930 almost 14 million households had radios; that brought the ratio up to about one in every two. By 1950, at least one radio could be found in virtually every household in the country, as well as in about half the cars on the road. Soon after, cordless, monaural, battery-operated sets, known as "transistor radios," were introduced. The sight of people walking around in public spaces listening to electronic earpieces became commonplace; random urban contact would never fully recover. By the end of the twentieth century, if an individual did not have round-the-clock access to broadcasting – at home, on foot, on the road, in a hospital bed, in the waiting room of a muffler repair shop or a doctor's office – an American might be tempted to ask, "Why not?"

What was so attractive about this new medium? What *is* so attractive about new media? How did radio manage in a matter of a few decades to develop from a rarefied instrument of international commerce and war – distant from the lives of all but a tiny technocratic elite – into a perceived personal necessity for individuals of nearly all social classes and subcultures?

The passionate embrace of radio in the 1920s provided a model that electronic communication and culture companies would find reliable for the balance of the twentieth century. Generations of new-tech communications hardware were continually being added to the American home in the years following the success of radio: television; stereo component systems (including FM radio tuners); reel-to-reel audiotape for home recording; long-playing records; color television; audiotape cassettes; VCRs; laser discs; compact discs; fax machines; cable TV; personal satellite dishes; DVDs; plasma monitors, and the others added since the writing of this book.

A close analogy to the mass diffusion of broadcast radio in the 1920s can be found in the spread of the internet-capable home computer in the 1990s. In both cases, recently established military-industrial processes yielded miniaturized byproducts that were mass-produced for sale as home appliances. Older companies, notably IBM and Xerox, held relevant patents and had the resources to dominate home computing from the start. They failed to do this, however, because, like David Sarnoff's bosses at RCA in 1916, they could see no reason why tens of millions of people would want such an appliance. Furthermore, they failed to understand that a pre-existing "reason" was not nearly so important in considering this diversification as the desire held by most people for novel, personalized sources of information and culture. Reason, with the help of a good advertising campaign, would take care of itself.

Newer companies, such as Apple (hardware) and America Online (software), better understood the lessons of twentieth-century American media culture and rose from thin circuits to become powerhouses. The user-group for home computers, like the user-group for broadcast radio, grew rapidly, reaching a point at which non-commercial uses of the newly massified medium were marginalized by the requirements of commercial sponsorship (as in the US) or by state subsidization and control (as in China).

Broadcasting: Love It or Need It?

Can we find in humanity a deep, structural desire for what broadcasting delivered to it a century ago? Can we identify a need that precedes its actual invention and goes to the heart of pre-industrial experience? As is so often the case with human inventions, a fantasy of self-empowerment initiates a process of toolmaking.

The arts and literatures of antiquity are full of all kinds of transcendent fantasies: human beings flying through the air, knocking down mountains or buildings, living beneath the sea, and so on. Sooner or later the hungers to fulfill these visions were realized by toolmakers as airplanes, bulldozers, submarines and other rationally constructed machines. Among these dreams of the supernatural-made-natural, perhaps none is more significant to our current evolution than communication by means that transcend normal modes of transportation.[1]

In the Old Testament, when God *tells* Adam not to eat the forbidden fruit, is the Almighty offering a PSA (public service announcement) that the listener would have done well to heed?[2] When Jacob dreams of a wrestling match with an angel (a wrestling match, we might add, whose outcome had already been predetermined) are we already on the way to Worldwide Wrestling Entertainment? Where did Noah get his weather? While voices and visions have throughout history landed their viewers and listeners in mental institutions, in some instances they have provided

A BURNING BUSH?

blueprints for the construction of new civilizations. To this way of thinking, the broadcasting industry did not create a need for radio and television, but instead answered needs – or stumbled upon answers to needs – that had been evolving in the human personality since walking upright became *de rigueur*. Broadcasting entered people's lives offering the personalized companionship of a higher power. For the lonely, silence became an option, ceding its ability to deafen to radio transmitters.

When people experienced what broadcasting could do, they would not let it go. One 1927 poll found that more Americans would rather give up indoor plumbing than their radios. By 1932 more than half the money spent on furniture in the United States was spent on the huge radios that became dominant pieces in American living rooms.[3]

Radio (and its quick improvement to television) offered easy access to a living, speaking higher consciousness, and in that sense it has provided its audience with some of the comforts of religion, without making any inscrutable demands. William Fore, a Methodist minister who for many years headed the National Council of Churches Broadcasting and Film Commission, suggests in his book *Television and Religion* that broadcasting, whether by design or coincidence, has subsumed many of the traditional functions of religion by offering its congregation a picture of the world (an *imago mundi*, to use an old religious term), and by defining how life in that world might be properly lived.[4]

Like the Bible, television offers self-definition by offering information to its followers on who they are, what their purpose is, how they should and should not behave, and how life can be satisfying. In both media, historical events and narratives are the primary rhetorical modes for making points. TV packages the former as The News and the latter as genre drama. If the Bible is the medium of record for Christianity, TV is the medium of record for a faith we might call Consumerism.

The voice of broadcasting, which first penetrated the homes of Americans during what historians call "the Jazz Age," assumed an intimacy with the listener close enough to comment on the odor of the breath or body, and yet, in a split-second segue, it could demonstrate the sweeping superhuman power of describing what was going on in the farthest reaches of the world. The voice brought stimulating and sedative waves of instant entertainment: music, drama, and snappy patter. The distant gods and goddesses of the cinema descended from the silver screen, spoke of their lives, and invited the listener to pay money to see them and to share their joy in consuming brand-name products.

Commercial broadcasting made many suggestions to the listener, but it did not argue or humiliate in any direct way. It informed and educated, but did not castigate or punish. You could have it when you wanted it and make it go away when you weren't in the mood. No matter how loudly or garishly a broadcasting appliance squawked or glared, you could pull the plug on it, and yet it would be

Pat Robertson, host of *The 700 Club*

A BURNING BUSH?

"I think, without question, through the Christian Broadcasting Network, we are seeing the fulfillment of this mandate of Jesus Christ: 'Go unto all the world and teach all nations, teaching them to observe all things which the Lord commanded you.' We now at CBN are operating in about a hundred and sixty-five countries, in as many as fifty or sixty different languages. Our audiences overseas are absolutely enormous. We produce local programs. We have programs for children. . . . I'm talking about tens of millions of people who are making decisions. It staggers the imagination. . . . We're not in some religious ghetto or some little tiny cable channel. Our programs go out into the mainstream. The people are so enthusiastic. People say, 'You're telling us about God. You're bringing us the Bible. You're praying for us. You love us. We're so grateful for what you're doing.' It's very heartening."

Pat Robertson, interviewed by David Marc, Virginia Beach, Virginia, February 16, 2000. Audiotape and transcription, oral history collections, Center for the Study of Popular Television, Syracuse University Library. Copyright Syracuse University 2000. This interview was made possible with funds provided by the Lilly Endowment Inc. Photographs courtesy of Syracuse University Library.

SIDEBAR 3.1

there for you without complaint the next time you summoned it. "Don't you dare touch that dial!" announcers have been playfully warning listeners since the advent of commercial radio. But the listener knows this is a lighthearted caveat. Go ahead and channel surf to your heart's delight. There is no retribution to suffer. Broadcasters want you to have fun. What's more, they even tell you how. Radio was the first reliable non-print, non-church connection to a great social construction called "society."

The Christian Bible is divided into two sequential texts, and there are significant differences in communication metaphors between the two. The Old Testament is replete with post-telegraphic communication imagery suggestive of early radio in that God speaks to individuals. The Old Testament's first book, Genesis, the kick-off for Jewish, Christian, and Islamic monotheism,[5] tells how God, presumably far away and without the aid of carrier pigeons, Western Union, AT&T, or the internet, instructs an individual, Abraham, to kill his only son as a proof of obedience. Abraham responds to the message by taking his boy to the altar and preparing to do as he has been told in the message. In a surprise ending, however, God reverses his original order and tells Abraham not to do it. Like the Emergency Broadcast System, it was only a test.[6] More episodes follow.

How, a secular humanist communications scholar might ask, did God communicate with Abraham? Theologians are likely to answer that this process is beyond human understanding because God is omnipotent. What is striking is that omnipotence is demonstrated by a process so similar to modern electronic communication.

In the New Testament the broadcasting metaphor goes beyond God's point-to-point messages to chosen individuals and becomes massified. Jesus, live on Earth, instructs his human disciples to preach the Gospel to every creature in every corner of the planet. In practical terms this is a feat not achievable without broadcasting and the other media that have followed. Pat Robertson, founder of the Christian Broadcasting Network, cites this biblical injunction as the inspiration for his rejection of a traditional theater-like pulpit in favor of worldwide satellite television operations. The role of television in the divine plan is crucial.

In 1925, as the first inklings of the power of radio were revealing themselves in the profits of advertising, Bruce Barton, a founder of the BBD&O advertising agency, wrote a best-selling novel, *The Man Nobody Knows*, in which he depicted Christianity itself as a pioneering advertising venture.[7] Jesus of Nazareth had, after all, repackaged the demographically tribal monotheism of the Hebrews into a commodity tailored for a worldwide general market. He went through the head-hunting process to recruit appropriate staff, and sent them forth to move the merchandise. "To create any sort of a reception for a new idea," wrote Barton in reference to the preaching of the Gospel, "involves a vast, expensive and well-organized machinery of propaganda."[8] In essence, Barton proudly depicts the Church as an advertising agency that must service a divine account. In the New Testament, a human elite is mandated to transmit information to the rest of humanity. After two millennia, a worldwide broadcasting system is finally in place to get the job done.

One reading of the Bible suggests that perhaps the human affinity for broadcasting grows out of an age-old visionary dream of information moving invisibly through the air, and the belief that the ability to move information in this way is a direct manifestation of divine power. But if the feat of broadcasting is so awe-inspiring as to insinuate the divine, does content really matter that much in people's acceptance of it?

A content-based explanation for the human acceptance – dare we call it love? – of broadcasting gives primary credit to the specific way in which the invention was handled and cultivated by individuals and institutions. Was it the actual programming that made radio so loved? Was it the hummable music of the commercial jingle? The instant emotional morass of the soap opera? The banter of the sitcom? The moral retributions of the cop show? The omniscient rush of The News? The pathos of medical drama?

A new class of merchant princes, ideologically free of the formal constraints of traditional European art and aesthetics, commissioned whole new genres of rhetoric and drama for broadcasting. The responses of the marketplace, rather than the judgments of canon-oriented elites, emerged as the standards by which the success of works was gauged, thus giving shape to the culture of the twentieth century and beyond. A content-based explanation holds that Americans loved radio (and television and their electronic culture in general) not because they necessarily had a need that these media filled, but because these media (or "The Media" as they came to be called) courted and pleased them so.

Social and psychological changes came with the advent of broadcasting, including new advantages for the classes that made the masses massive. People whose poverty – whose very clothes – forbade them from entering the theater or the concert hall suddenly had professionally produced music and drama brought right to them in the tenement, the barn, and the backroom of the shop. They could even change the channel if they were not pleased by what was put before them, and when they did, their social superiors were forced to take notice. People who could not read a newspaper were made privy to national and international current affairs. Millions of immigrants, born and bred at the lower end of Old World caste systems, found themselves, quite suddenly, the objects of persuasion in America, courted by the New World entrepreneur-aristocrats who sat atop the masscult pyramid. While there is much evidence that intellectuals felt put-upon by the relentless commercial pitchmanship of radio, there is every reason to believe that the masses in their new role as mass audience were pleased to find themselves in

"I don't think you can ever underestimate the American public's desire for more video choices. That appetite seems to expand. It's peculiar in some respects, because the number of channels that people actually watch is no more than ten or twelve, even as the number of channels available to them may expand well beyond that. But the perception of value that people find comes from having all that expanded choice. It is something that consumers seem to continue to believe is a very positive development. More choice, more offerings, is good. Despite the fact that you may watch a limited number of those, the fact that there is more choice out there seems to drive an awful lot."

Thomas S. Rogers, interviewed by David Marc, New York City, March 10, 1998. Audiotape and transcription, Steven H. Scheuer Collection in Television History, Center for the Study of Popular Television, Syracuse University Library. Copyright Syracuse University 1999. Rogers was instrumental in launching cable operations for NBC television.

3.2 SIDEBAR

demand for something other than the sweatshop, the coal mine, or the army. These were pleasures of the text that few critics of broadcasting had ever imagined, much less experienced or understood.

A Vertical System of Culture

Radio broadcasting was so loved that almost immediately upon delivery from the lab it established its content as the nucleus of an American national culture, something that many historians suggest did not exist at all previously. Like the flash diffusion of the internet via home computers in the 1990s, broadcasting via home radios presented sudden and extraordinary opportunities for both the American business and artistic communities.

What kind of programming could be created to assemble formidable mass audiences? The nation-state identities that had emerged from the ruins of the ancient empires had, up to this point, been defined by broad traits, such as a common language, shared religion, and political unity. But in terms of the arts, class differentiation had remained the rule. The aristocracies of European nations shared a transnational "high culture" with each other. This was true in virtually every area of cultural life, and it was a circumstance that seemed guaranteed by disparities of wealth and education.

The advertising agencies that began producing American radio programs in the 1920s not only failed to respect conventional class boundaries, they were bound and determined to leap over any traditional cultural indicators that stood in the way of increasing audience size. Not even such powerfully distinctive characteristics as religion, ethnicity, or regionalism were allowed to limit the possibilities of the ratings. No area of cultural life was presumed safe from what proponents hailed as the new inclusive democratic culture of the radio – and what critics feared as the leveling of all standards. "I don't think anybody knew what the word 'demographic' meant," said Dr. Frank Stanton, in recalling how the listener was imagined and counted in the early days of network radio. A pioneering audience measurement theorist who left a faculty position at Ohio State University to work for CBS, Stanton eventually became first president of the company's television network.[9]

As we have seen, David Sarnoff had been quick to understand the significant role that broadcasting could play in the everyday lives of millions. However, even he was not prepared at first for the remarkable revelation that music, drama, information, and even the vocal styles of announcers might be so easily accepted and shared by what amounted to 90 percent or more of the American public on a daily basis. When Sarnoff put RCA's National Broadcasting Company on the air in 1927 as the world's first commercial broadcasting network, he launched not one but two national chains: the Blue Network, aimed downscale; and the Red Network, aimed up. However, differences in content between the two NBC audio networks blurred as the 1930s wore on. By the time the Roosevelt administration forced RCA to divest itself of one of the two, the differences in content were negligible. Ironically, the slicing up of the national audience into demographic slivers, which would occur in the cable TV era of the 1980s and 1990s, would prove a far more time-consuming and complicated task than the assembling of that mass audience did some sixty years earlier.

Who could have imagined that a professional college graduate and an illiterate day-laborer might both sit still, same time/same station, to listen to the big band music of the Dorsey Brothers or to follow the adventures of *Jack Armstrong, the All-American Boy*? Or that Philadelphia lawyers and Colorado ranchers might both get their information about the European crisis each day from the same news source? But then again who could have imagined all these folks might get up during the commercial to have a Coke?

Totalitarian political parties salivated at radio power, seeing in it a mechanism of mass control that could bypass formal education, religion, and even local social tradition. Fascists made especially effective use of it in Europe before drowning in their own bloodbath. Communists would ultimately forfeit their empire in part through their inept handling of it. In the end it was American advertising agencies who understood the possibilities most fully, and who addressed the particulars in creating mass culture.

Old-line conservatives fussed over the collapse of tradition in the face of the new pop arts of broadcasting.[10] Socialists, impatiently clamoring for capitalism to collapse, failed to notice that the industrial system of the US was being restructured for a new economy of all-out consumerism, which they were unprepared to understand, much less overthrow. Entrepreneurs looked at the sales reports produced by their broadcasting campaigns and seized the opportunity to build the walls and doors that would allow them to become the gatekeepers of the Age of Information.

American business bet its future on the proposition that a highly educated and well-to-do elite could build a communication system capable of successfully commanding the attention of millions of people, most of whom were far less educated or cultured than they. With radio broadcasting, hardware had become the easy part. But a difficult task remained: software. Could writers, composers, journalists, editors, and other artists and artisans supply potent programming for daily use to get the most out of the broadcasting mainframe's capabilities?

The historical precedents for entertaining hundreds of millions of people as "one big audience" were few, but the previous two most successful efforts at this were very American: the mass-circulation newspaper and the Hollywood movie.[11] By the time that American broadcasting reached its full flower in the pre-cable television era, it had eclipsed and encompassed both.

Compatible Software

"Radio was a terrific stimulator of a capacity for fantasy – compared to television."
Peggy Charren, Founder, Children's Action for Television[12]

"You pictured people when listening to radio. But that happens less and less now. So asking TV audiences to imagine something on their own . . . it comes hard for them."
Betty White, radio and TV sitcom actress[13]

The reign of radio as the central distribution point of American national culture (the reign, that is, of radio-without-TV) was short but, according to many who lived through it, sweet. The feature of pre-visual broadcasting that seems to be most fondly remembered, even revered, by its survivors is the ability of purely aural drama to stimulate the listener to construct a kind of theater of the mind. Radio transmission provided story, voices, and sound effects. It was up to the listener, however, to animate all that by creating faces, movement, scenery, and color.

Thus radio, as a dramatic medium, has an interactive characteristic that is lacking in theater, film, and television. This probably helps explain why its period of dominance is remembered so warmly, rather than as, say, the first great penetration

SIDEBAR 3.3

William Link and his partner Richard Levinson collaborated to create, write, and produce dozens of popular TV series and films, including such *fin-de-siècle* hits as *Columbo* and *Murder, She Wrote*. Link actually credits listening to radio drama with helping him prepare for his life as a collaborative television writer:

"I remember listening to *I Love a Mystery* when I was like six or seven years old and it would scare the bejesus out of me. Radio was an unleashing of the imagination because *you* would supply [the images]. On radio you heard the voices and some rather cheap sound effects, but you created that whole world, which is what you do when you write a short story, or a novel or a screenplay."

William Link, interviewed by David Marc at his home in Beverly Hills, California, November 15, 1996. Audiotape and transcription, Steven H. Scheuer Collection in Television History, Center for the Study of Popular Television, Syracuse University Library. Copyright Syracuse University 1999.

of electronic culture into the privacy of home and family. What could have been more user-friendly? But if the pre-TV radio years indeed constituted a golden age, as writer Norman Corwin points out, it was perhaps "the shortest golden age in history."[14] Corwin, like Betty White quoted above, grew up with radio in the 1930s and 1940s. They both went on to work in the medium during the glory days when it stood smack-dab at the center of the American consciousness industry.

By the mid-1950s, however, both the radio performer and the radio writer had little choice but to follow their audiences to television. Just as the flourishing art of the silent film fell sudden fatal victim to the hi-tech juggernaut of talking pictures in the late 1920s, the art of radio drama succumbed to TV. With so much money at stake, there is no room for sentiment in the Darwinian jungle of the American culture industry. What survives of American radio drama requires taxpayer support, for the most part, in the form of reruns and rare new productions on public radio stations.

Though now reduced to a supplemental weapon in the entertainment-industrial complex's arsenal of communication systems, radio remains with us. The national obsessions with automobile transportation and round-the-clock, demographically specific advertising have forestalled the utter abandonment of the medium, as was the case of the silent cinema. For the most part radio has evolved into a thoroughly formatted medium, dedicated to a narrow band of musical tastes and rhetorical mindsets. There are, however, several roles that post-TV radio has carved out for itself that are worth noting.

AM call-up talk shows constitute one of the few electronic soapboxes which citizens – other than the usual two dozen professional TV "pundits" – can use to express themselves via the electronic apparatus of the masscom system. The opinions of lunatics, paranoids, and the thoroughly misinformed and uninformed flow through the air, mixing gingerly with those of the thoughtful, the compassionate, and the educated. This aural collage, however, is more often entertaining than distressing. There comes a sense while listening to these programs that the body politic of American democracy is actively getting some much-needed exercise in a culture where election day is ignored by more than half the population.

Radio news reporting, especially of the commercial variety, is not nearly so lively. The "all-news" commercial stations, many of them the old AM properties of Westinghouse and CBS, rarely offer anything other than a loop of 30-second "capsules" that are little more than disembodied aural headlines. Some radio stations just play the sound portion of TV newscasts. The great exception to this decline of radio news, and to the decline of radio in general, is National Public Radio. NPR, which went on the air in 1969, is the publicly supported radio network that America never had during the medium's "golden age." Much to its credit, it has taken up the work of developing the potential of radio as something other than an also-ran commercial medium which might sell acne medicine to teenagers and aspirin to seniors.

The struggle to create and practice vital standards of journalistic excellence and ethics in radio, which reached a crescendo of intensity in CBS Radio's Second World War coverage, was long ago abandoned (on both radio and TV) by all of the commercial broadcasting companies. Meanwhile, NPR news programs, such as *All Things Considered* and *Morning Edition*, offer higher IQ at a lower decibel rate, serving an influential niche audience whose attention span has been said to run into the minutes. For this group, top-heavy with owners of Swedish cars, parents of children who play soccer, and nerdocrats, NPR fills in the void for the modern managing class that automobile commuting created in newspaper reading.

Though traditional American broadcasting commercials are banned on NPR stations, public radio in America is by no means "commercial-free." Understated "announcements" of "underwriter support" are offered at the beginning and end of programs. The revenue obtained from these faux commercials, however, is not enough to pay the bills. Stations, most of which are already subsidized by universities or other non-profit institutions, must beg money directly from their listeners in (unbearable) pledge-a-thons. Federal money comes to NPR through the Corporation for Public Broadcasting. This process requires Congressional hearings that are even more unbearable.

The effect of all this nickel-and-diming is to leave the spectrum of ideas available on public radio only marginally wider than the thin duct made available by its commercial cousins. The handful of radio stations in the country playing classical, jazz, bluegrass and other sub-pop music forms are, with few exceptions, public stations. An occasional radio play is even produced. But a listener interested in a political opinion outside what is commercially permitted must forget American radio (see chapter 8).[15]

In the larger history of human communication, radio is not likely to be remembered much for its unique aesthetics. However, its place is secure as the enabler of the marriage of technology and marketing that occurred during the period when radio was the state-of-the-art tool of mass communication. Radio was the testing ground for experiments in national marketing whose success would shape the development of the US for the coming century. With the launch of NBC in the later 1920s, radio began the work of making one large market of an American empire of regions, ethnicities and races. Without the advertising opportunities created by the building of these commercial communication networks, the uniform fast-food outlets and chain megastores that have replaced old-fashioned cities and towns would not have been possible.

The radio network was made possible by a synthesis of emerging capabilities. First, the introduction of wireless broadcasting technology allowed individual transmitting stations to penetrate as many homes as possible within the radius of

NORMAN LLOYD

Norman Lloyd's career as an actor, director, and producer spans seven decades and four dramatic media: theater, film, radio, and television. He appeared in a 1939 episode of *Streets of New York*, which was among the first television programs ever made for the public; produced *Alfred Hitchcock Presents*, a filmed drama anthology during the 1950s; and appeared in such later prime-time series as *St. Elsewhere* and *The Practice*. Here he responds to a question about the relationship of performance and medium.

DAVID MARC. Do you think young actors who begin their careers in television today are missing something important by not starting out on the stage?

NORMAN LLOYD. What is lost, first, is speech. The actor has lost poetry. The theater is a medium of poetry, at its greatest, at its best. It is a medium of words. Of course, today, with our being so acclimatized to graphic and visual elements, we expect more in the theater in the way of sex and lights than when I started. But, on the other hand, what has never changed is the importance of words, the poetry of the theater. That is what an actor in television loses. He also loses that most remarkable of all things: immediacy and contact with an audience. That is thrilling. When it is working between you and the audience, you realize that this thrill may have been why you went into the profession.

DM. Does the audience lose something as well?

NL. Theater – it was part of your life. You had to have two things, theater and education. You didn't need the automobile. I don't think television has an equivalent purpose in people's lives today. Yes, they watch television a lot, because it is something that keeps people quiet. But it doesn't have the same relation to the audience as the one that I've described.

Norman Lloyd was interviewed by David Marc, Los Angeles, March 17, 1997. Audiotape and transcription, Steven H. Scheuer Collection in Television History, Center for the Study of Popular Television, Syracuse University Library. Copyright Syracuse University 1999.

their power. Then the older technology of wired telephones increased radio's capability geometrically by linking those transmitting stations in a chain from coast to coast. The result was a hardware that made it possible for millions of spatially divided people to receive the same message at the same time. Depending on software selection, listeners could be re-identified as an audience, a congregation, or even a nation.

Theaters and concert halls could produce audiences numbering in the hundreds; arenas and stadiums could produce them in the tens of thousands. Books could claim readership in the millions; a movie, by increments, could gain an audience in the tens of millions. But broadcasting did something new. Scores of millions of people could be assembled, "same time, same station," to attend a single communication.

Network capability concentrated a degree of cultural power in the hands of the new communication elite that rivaled that of the Catholic Church before the Reformation. Radio could create significance merely by noticing things. It could confer obscurity by turning a deaf ear. The voice of American radio became in effect the sound of the reasonable center, a report from reality, a message from a higher power on the subject of what's what in the world. It could speak in this voice while describing Germany invading Poland or selling a remedy for planter's warts.

The nation of radio owners constituted a gargantuan user-group, larger than that of literacy, with the added feature of simultaneous attendance. What kind of software might appeal to such a multitude? Up until the birth of the radio network, programming had been almost an afterthought. Like most new media before or since, radio began its life by functioning as an improved distribution system for existing media: the radio *play*; the radio *news*; the radio *sermon*; the radio *concert*.

By the early 1950s, less than thirty years after the NBC and CBS networks went on the air, American radio had developed a powerful portfolio of successful genres: the sitcom, the cop show, the medical show, the soap opera, the comedy-variety show, the daily news program, the news documentary, the children's program, and so on. As a part of that process, the significant "day parts" had been isolated for optimal marketing purposes: prime time, daytime, Saturday morning, early morning, late-night, and so on. The consciousness-making factory of Consumer Society had put its assembly line in place. And then, quite suddenly, it was all over (for radio, that is, not the factory). The orders came from above. Radio was abandoned to the fate of a cottage medium, a way of covering drivers during their journeys between television sets.

Henry Morgenthau, son of the Secretary of the Treasury of the United States during the Franklin D. Roosevelt administration, relates this story of his attempt to get into the radio business at the dawn of the Television Era.

HENRY MORGENTHAU. I got organized with a friend of mine. We were both young veterans [of the Second World War] at the time. We started to make an application for a radio station. We went quite far on it. You had to have a site for the antenna. I remember, we got permission to have one on top of the Carlisle Hotel [in New York]. Then, as time went on, it seemed like it was too much to organize and finance. My father, who of course knew everybody, including General Sarnoff, sent me to see General Sarnoff. I have a memory . . . of walking down endless corridors, sort of like approaching the Sun King at Versailles, and meeting Sarnoff and talking to him briefly. He said that he thought going into radio was the worst possible thing to do.

DAVID MARC. Did he mean that he thought radio was going to disappear because of television?

HM. I can't say that. But I do remember that he said, "Get into television!" Sarnoff was really tremendously farsighted about television. In fact, I read a talk that he gave [on it] in 1929 at Harvard Business School.

Henry Morgenthau, interviewed by David Marc, Cambridge, Massachusetts, May 6, 1998. Audiotape and transcription, Steven H. Scheuer Collection in Television History, Center for the Study of Popular Television, Syracuse University Library. Copyright Syracuse University 1999.

3.4 SIDEBAR

Notes

1   See Jacques Ellul, *The Technological Society* (New York: Knopf, 1965).

2   See Genesis 2: 17.

3   Both these statistics are taken from the documentary *Empire of the Air: The Men Who Made Radio*, produced by Ken Burns (Alexandria, VA: PBS Video; Radio Pioneers Film Project, Inc., ca. 1991).

4   William Fore, *Television and Religion: The Shaping of Faith, Values and Culture* (Minneapolis: Augsburg Publishing House, 1987).

5   Monotheistic religions believe in God as a single being. Polytheistic religions, by contrast, believe in the simultaneous existence of many gods.

6   See Karen Armstrong, *A History of God* (New York: Knopf, 1994), especially pp. 13–15.

7   Bruce Barton, *The Man Nobody Knows* (New York: Bobbs-Merrill, 1925). The book went into its twenty-fourth printing in 1984.

8   Ibid., p. 63.

9   Frank Stanton, interviewed by David Marc, May 21, 1999. Steven H. Scheuer Collection in Television History, Center for the Study of Popular Television. Copyright Syracuse University, 1999. In the 1930s Stanton devised many of the techniques that remain in use in the twenty-first century to measure audience preference and size.

10 See T. S. Eliot, *Christianity and Culture* (New York: Harcourt, Brace, 1960), especially "Notes Towards the Definition of Culture," for an example of the rejection of popular culture by traditionalist conservatives.

11 The development of the motion picture industry is historically close to the development of the broadcasting industry. However, the Hollywood film clearly precedes radio in the chronology of mass entertainment forms. The silent film, for example, was drawing millions before commercial broadcasting even existed. The great leap forward in attendance and profitability occasioned by sound film was well underway during the last three years of the 1920s, even as the radio networks were attempting to invent themselves.

12 Peggy Charren, interviewed by David Marc, Boston, May 5, 1998. Audiotape and transcription, Steven H. Scheuer Collection in Television History, Center for the Study of Popular Television. Copyright Syracuse University 1999.

13 Betty White, interviewed by David Marc, Los Angeles, April 29, 1997. Audiotape and transcription. Steven H. Scheuer Collection in Television History, Center for the Study of Popular Television. Copyright Syracuse University 1999.

14 Ken Burns, producer, *Empire of the Air.*

15 The exceptions to this rule are the radio stations licensed to the Pacifica Foundation, which is dedicated to free speech. The Pacifica Stations also, unfortunately, prove the rule.

~ 4 ~
STAGING AND SCREENING

Sets

Television was introduced to most of America during a ten-year period beginning in about 1948. Shopping malls as we know them did not yet exist, and most retail businesses were still located in urban business districts with only limited parking and along small-town main streets. Given such primitive retailing conditions, it was not unusual to see a crowd of people standing in the street in front of an appliance dealership watching TV through the store window.

These impromptu sidewalk audiences laughed, applauded, and even heckled the entertainment, with new viewers leaving and joining the group casually at intervals. Were they watching the commercials? As had been the case with the introduction of radio some twenty-five years earlier, this was not yet important. The first task in the launch of any new medium – radio, TV, videogames, desktop computers, cellular phones – is to sell receiving equipment. The significant commercial on early TV was the television selling itself.

Television seemed to be taking form as a kind of social activity indoors as well. Bar owners, seeing the advantages of offering legal "free entertainment" to their customers, actually used it to get people *out* of their homes. This is a phenomenon that would be repeated with the introduction of other new-tech features over the years, including color broadcast, widescreen TV, and satellite cable. The first sets in bars were usually installed on high-up shelves or ceiling brackets, as this allowed for convenient viewing without disruption of drinking. Operating an overhead set in a bar during the late 1940s and early 1950s required a degree of physical labor. Bartenders had to be ready to climb atop the bar at a moment's notice to shift the antenna with changes in the wind, or just to change the channel (where there was more than one). Hotels established "TV rooms" near or even in their lobbies as a cheap new automated social activity to offer guests, some of whom did not yet have televisions in their homes. Motels, usually lacking lobbies, were among the first lodgings to install sets right inside individual rooms.

Bringing television home was quite an expensive proposition at first. In 1947, with the average price of a brand-new house under $10,000, the average price of a new black-and-white, manually operated, non-cable-ready set (and of course there was no other kind) averaged about $279. Sets could be high-maintenance items as well. Some had cooling systems and needed to be watered from time to time. Anyone who could afford a television also needed a place to put it. While screens tended to be tiny by today's standards, the innards of a set contained an extensive maze of glass tubes and connectors that blew up the unit to the size of a substantial chest of draws.

Since many of the radio sets in American living-rooms were themselves substantial pieces of furniture, the first micro-skirmishes between the two communication media were battles for domestic space on a house-to-house basis. Given the fact that the same companies were manufacturing both televisions and radios, it is not surprising that radios got much smaller very quickly during this period. Those people with the money, space, and desire to put sets in their homes soon found themselves enjoying the same kind of dubious popularity as swimming pool owners. As one's neighbors bought their own television sets, one might learn who one's real friends were.

Whatever problems set ownership presented, the vast majority of Americans eagerly made the plunge by cash or credit.[1] By 1960, setlessness was a condition afflicting under 13 percent of the US population. Television refuseniks came largely from two groups: (1) an educated elite of ideological opponents of the medium, and (2) the utterly poverty-stricken. Resistance, as aliens liked to tell Earthlings in the popular sci-fi movies of the day, was futile.

As set ownership rose toward virtual saturation throughout the 1950s, TV-viewing in the streets declined, though it would make a comeback of sorts in the 1980s with the installation of giant-screen televisions in public places, such as ballparks and city squares. But for the time being people went home to watch, spending less time on their front porches and stoops, or at movie theaters or other civic entertainment venues. At the same time mass automobile ownership increased throughout the decade, and this too reinforced the desocialization of daily life by removing people from streetcars, buses, and trains, and leaving them in their private vehicles with their radios.

Cities, which had been centers of social activity by design and development, found themselves abandoned by millions of middle-class people who came to see them as user-unfriendly wastelands where you had to pay for everything from parking to shopping to an evening's entertainment. American society was becoming a "lonely crowd," as sociologist David Reisman suggested in the title of his 1953 book.[2]

However, as judged by their actions, most Americans either craved or loved the privacy afforded them in a life shaped by physical movement in cars and psychological removal through watching television. The new Interstate Highway System and the new television networks emerged as the corporeal and aesthetic circulatory systems of the American body politic.

Even *inside* the home, this pattern of movement from social engagement to self-engagement was repeated. Distinctions between such familiar spatial designations as "living-room," "den," and "finished basement" melted in the family's quest to fulfill its viewing needs. This was especially true in smaller dwellings, where the television could be heard, if not seen, in every corner of the home. The frozen TV dinner in a throwaway aluminum container was introduced to eliminate such impediments to viewing time as cooking and cleaning up. Family eye contact suffered as heads rotated toward the point of reception.

Yet, at least during these early stages of televisual cultural reform, the family usually sat together in the same room to view, approximating the old notions of both a family activity and membership in an audience. Marshall McLuhan, who was earning the distinction of becoming the first "media critic," described television in the 1950s as an "electronic hearth," a kind of proto-cyberworld fireplace, around which families were gathering during this new stage of post-industrial existence. It should also be noted that he is credited with coining the term "the media," which has become so essential to describing modern experience.[3]

However, this bit of familial social cohesion turned out to be a temporary feature of the broadcast-only period. With only three or four channels available, each offering content almost indistinguishable from the other, cultural compromises had to be made if one wished to watch television at all. A viewer wishing to see Elvis Presley or the Beatles or the Rolling Stones on *The Ed Sullivan Show* would have to put up with an appearance of the Bolshoi Ballet or the song stylings of Steve Lawrence and Eydie Gorme to get there, and vice versa for the fans of the other acts. The spread of satellite cable in the 1980s ended this by bringing dozens of new channels into the home, many of them targeted at individual family members to the exclusion of others. Family members began to scatter to their private demographic corners of the HUT.[4] Whereas, during the Broadcast Era, families had pondered the wisdom of buying a "second set," it had gradually become evident by the Cable Era that no member of the family would settle for less than a personal monitor, or perhaps two, under his or her full control.

Getting with the Program

Much of the programming on early television, especially before about 1955, was adapted from two tried-and-true media: radio and theater. The adaptation of

GORE VIDAL

Gore Vidal's novels and essays have made him one of the best-known American writers in the world, but few of his readers know that he began his career writing television plays during the late 1940s and early 1950s.

"There were seven ad agencies [controlling television] at that time. I remember being lectured by McCann Erickson, which was a deeply Roman Catholic, rightwing sort of outfit. They said, ideally, a play has got to be interesting, otherwise they switch off and then they'll miss the commercials, which, of course, is where all the creative passion has gone – into the commercials. It must be interesting enough so that they'll still be tuned in for the commercial, but it must not be *too* interesting, or the audience will not like the interruptions of the commercials. This is the first time in world history that you were asked, deliberately, to be mediocre. Now, we often achieve that on our own. But to really have this written in letters of fire: Do not be too interesting . . ."

Gore Vidal was interviewed by Steven H. Scheuer, Los Angeles, March 8, 1996. Videotape and transcription, Steven H. Scheuer Collection in Television History, Center for the Study of Popular Television, Syracuse University Library. Copyright Syracuse University 1999.

popular radio programs for television was natural enough for the broadcast networks; the networks and the advertising agencies, which produced most of the radio shows, were simply diversifying or technologically embellishing the broadcasting business. However, the choice of theater over film as a model for early TV production was a more complicated one. The two major broadcasting companies, NBC and CBS, did not want the Hollywood movie studios owning competitive television networks, and so they fought to identify television as something other than an outlet for film. They chose live theater as the mold out of which TV drama would be fashioned. The theater model offered other advantages as well: plays were cheaper to produce than movies, they retained the aura of "live entertainment," and there was an enormous talent base of stage actors in New York City, the broadcasting industry's home base. Moreover, Broadway performers were used to making far less money than Hollywood movie stars.

ABBY MANN

Abby Mann wrote and produced "Judgment at Nuremberg," a teleplay concerning the Nazi war crime trials, for *Playhouse 90* (CBS, 1956–61), the last of the great early television drama anthology series. Though the film adaptation (with a screenplay written by Mann) is well remembered and revered, the original TV version is virtually forgotten and did not win many accolades. Mann offers an explanation here in this anecdote. What may seem like a quaint story of censorship from times past also contains something of a cautionary tale about the contemptuous attitude that many critics still reserve for television.

"I said to myself, '"Judgment at Nuremberg" will give them something to think about!' But it was not critically acclaimed and we didn't even get an Emmy nomination. One reason had to do with a line in the script: the convicted [Nazi] judge says to the American judge, 'I know I've done terrible things, but you must believe that all those millions of people winding up in gas ovens – I never knew it would come to that.' One of our sponsors was a gas company and they said, 'You can't say that about gas ovens.' So we changed the line to 'all those millions of people being killed.' But the story of the line change got out to the critics and instead of saying something about the important issues in 'Judgment at Nuremberg,' they said, 'The gas company pumped out those lines' – and that became the story."

Abby Mann was interviewed by Steven H. Scheuer, Los Angeles, September 27, 1997. Videotape and transcription, Steven H. Scheuer Collection in Television History, Center for the Study of Popular Television, Syracuse University Library. Copyright Syracuse University 1999.

Most prime-time network drama before 1955 was presented live in an *anthology* format. These series, with names like *Philco-Goodyear Playhouse* and *Ford Theater*, presented new dramas each week, with no continuing characters or plot lines. Everything was done to make the show seem more like the experience of seeing a play than going to the movies. For example writers, who were (and remain) virtually anonymous in movies and most electronic software, were featured in ads and promos for anthology presentations, much as playwrights were lauded on Broadway. Instead of scripts, they wrote "teleplays."

Another theater-derived genre prominent in early television was "comedy-variety." This too was presented live. Unlike the more prestigious teleplays, which approximated what was known as "legitimate" theater, TV comedy-variety owed its form to what was considered a "lower" form of theater art, vaudeville. Vaudeville had been the single most popular form of live theater before the advent of motion pictures. In contrast to stage plays, vaudeville shows had no single "story" to present. They consisted of various kinds of performing acts: singers, comedians, dancers, magicians, hypnotists, trained animals, contortionists, and even circus freaks.

The networks' strategy of presenting these forms of "live theater" rather than "movies at home" ended in the mid-1950s. The key event that would change the course of television's aesthetic development from a theatrical orientation toward film-based visions was integrally tied to the birth and survival of the third national television network, the American Broadcasting Company (ABC).

The Origins of ABC

NBC and CBS, as the two dominant commercial radio broadcasting corporations, understood earliest and most fully what kind of money was possible in commercial television, and how it might be made. For twenty years the two radio giants had been working in close partnership with the brain trust of Madison Avenue in the construction of a system of market research and all-out product promotion designed to maximize the consumption of goods and services as the basic marker of life experience. This cultural regime has continued without interruption and has since been successfully exported to much of the world.

David Sarnoff, who as head of RCA from the 1920s to the 1970s was privy to every nuance of television's technical development, came to see radio, even during the peak of its profitability, as a mere testing ground for what could be achieved with television. According to David Adams, an NBC executive who later became a member of the RCA board of directors, "Sarnoff looked upon [television] as a new and major development, larger than radio, and actively pushed NBC into television. Of course, RCA was a set manufacturer, so it profited from the rise of television and the expansion of television."[5] At CBS, William Paley chose his top marketing executive, Frank Stanton, to head up CBS's new television network.

As licensed radio broadcasters, Sarnoff, Paley, and their top managers had an inside understanding of government broadcasting regulations, something other entertainment companies, such as movie studios, publishers, and record companies, had little or no experience of. They would use this to great advantage in making things more difficult for any non-broadcasting companies that might try to get a piece of what they considered their exclusive pie (see sidebar).

Two factors creating artificial station scarcity

The freeze on new stations, 1948–1952

As of 1948, the Federal Communications Commission (FCC) had issued 108 licenses to operate television stations. The great majority of the license-holders were still in the process of building their transmitters. The networks themselves held five licenses each (the legal limit), and most of the other license-holders owned radio stations that were affiliated to either NBC or CBS, and were eager to continue their relationships with the nets in what promised to be an even more profitable industry.

NBC and CBS successfully lobbied the FCC in 1948 to impose a two-year freeze on the issuance of new station licenses so that certain technical problems, such as signal interference in some markets, could be worked out. In 1950, the networks convinced the FCC to extend the freeze for two more years. The result was to squash the attempts of other companies to start up television networks during this crucial period in the introduction of television.

Paramount Pictures (a movie studio), Zenith (an electronics manufacturer), and Skiatron (a market research company) all were forced to give up on their plans for new television networks because there were no new stations for them to operate or to affiliate with. Was a four-year moratorium on new stations justifiable in terms of the technical problems it was supposed to address? Or were these companies – and the viewing public – the victims of a business trust operating with government compliance?

RCA's UHF blackout

Another factor that limited new television stations and prevented the establishment of new networks even after the freeze had finally ended was RCA's refusal to manufacture sets that received the UHF band of stations. All of RCA's NBC stations were VHF stations (channels 2–13). The larger UHF band contained channels 14–81. As the largest manufacturer of televisions in America, the company effectively cut the number of channels that potential competitors might operate from 81 to 12. It was not until 1961, when Congress passed the All-Channel Receiver Bill, that UHF was fully opened up for use.

Another national radio company, the Mutual Broadcasting System (MBS), chose not to get into the TV business at all. While NBC and CBS were networks that owned radio stations, MBS was a network owned by radio stations, a kind of cooperative vehicle for the sharing of programming resources. As such, it lacked the central corporate authority and identity necessary to pursue a television presence. However, given the bankability of its "household name" brand, and the existence of its strong news division, MBS's decision appears, in retrospect, to have been shortsighted. Yet it is also possible that MBS, as a long-time competitor to NBC and CBS, knew just how difficult it would be to get into the television business.

The American Broadcasting Company was the newest and perhaps least prepared of the four national radio networks, but it decided that it would go into the television business. ABC had actually started out as a part of the RCA corporate empire. When RCA launched the National Broadcasting Company in 1927 it created two networks, the Red and the Blue, each with its own programming (see chapter 2). However, in 1943 the company was forced by a US government anti-trust action to divest itself of one of the two networks. The Blue Network became the American Broadcasting Company.

Today it is common for a single company to own dozens of radio and / or TV stations, as well as cable outlets and other mass communication businesses. So it may seem rather odd that RCA, the largest media conglomerate in the world at that time, should have been prevented from retaining ownership of a mere two radio networks. A knowledge of the political conditions under which the industry developed is essential to understanding how this came about.

During the period from 1920 to 1932, the key years during which the federal government defined the rights and responsibilities of radio broadcasters, three Republican administrations – of Harding, Coolidge, and Hoover – had been in office. In 1921, President Warren G. Harding appointed Herbert Hoover as Secretary of Commerce, and thus as the chief government regulator of radio (see chapter 2). An engineer by training, Hoover understood the need for uniform technical standards in the new medium. He called industry leaders to a meeting known as the Washington Radio Conference of 1922, where he presented a comprehensive plan covering such issues as channel assignment, transmission power, and bandwidth.[6]

Existing laws, however, were not sufficient to support Hoover's attempt at establishing rational standards for American radio. The Zenith Corporation, for example, refused to change the frequency of its Chicago station in accordance with the Hoover plan. Zenith's action was upheld by the US Supreme Court, and the radio industry was plunged into chaos, with new licensees setting up frequencies wherever they liked, and with stronger stations blasting weaker ones into oblivion at will. Gradually, however, there was a general recognition in the business community that the profit potentials of commercial radio were being seriously hamstrung by the lack of regulation. In a rare instance in American history, industry invited federal regulation.

In 1927, President Calvin Coolidge signed comprehensive legislation taking federal regulatory power away from commerce and giving it to a new, specially created body, the Federal Radio Commission (FRC). The FRC was successful in re-establishing the same standards that Hoover had proposed five years earlier at a second gathering, the Washington Radio Conference of 1927.

In 1928, Herbert Hoover was elected president. Though he had very serious misgivings about the likely cultural consequences of a radio system so thoroughly dominated by commercial interests (see chapter 2), he was, first and foremost, committed to a free-market economic philosophy that kept government away from business regulation as much as possible. When it became an indisputable fact on the ground that American radio would be principally an advertising business, he took no steps during his administration toward regulation of the radio industry, or any other (even after the stock market crash of 1929).

In 1932, with the nation deep in throes of the Great Depression, Franklin D. Roosevelt defeated Hoover. He was the first Democrat in the White House since KDKA had gone on the air. Unlike Hoover, FDR had committed himself to using the power of government to actively intervene in business affairs where he thought the nation's best interests were at stake. However, with national unemployment reaching upwards of 25 percent, the regulation of radio was not very high on the list of New Deal[7] priorities. Even so, over the course of Roosevelt's presidency, a number of significant steps were taken that culminated in NBC's forced divestiture of the Blue Network. The Communications Act of 1934 recognized the increasing importance of radio, telephone, and other growing public communication services (including the recently patented laboratory marvel known as television). The FRC was revamped and rechristened the Federal Communications Commission. Perhaps the FCC's most remarkable achievement was that it successfully imposed a rate reduction on AT&T's telephone service in 1939. But, as concerns television, its most significant contribution was *The Report on Chain Broadcasting*, released in 1941.

In effect the report said that RCA would have to get rid of one of its two NBC networks if it wished to remain in the broadcasting business. CBS, with only one national network, had less to lose, but with prospects for its wealth and power growing, the company did not want its future expansion hamstrung by any new FCC limitations. The two rivals cooperated in taking the case to federal court in 1941, hoping to have the Chain Broadcasting Report declared unconstitutional. The Mutual Broadcasting System saw advantages in limiting the size of its biggest competitors, and filed an *amicus* brief on behalf of the government position.

Even while the case was still in court, RCA began restructuring NBC for the likelihood of a defeat. First off, the Red and Blue networks were split into separate divisions. The Red Network had always been more profitable and so it would be the keeper. Beginning in late 1941, the name "Red Network" was dropped from station breaks, and it identified itself on the air as, simply, "NBC." Conversely the name "NBC" was dropped from station identification messages on the other service, which now announced itself as "the Blue Network." In 1943 the US Supreme Court ruled in favor of the FCC, and two months later NBC sold the Blue Network – including its o&o stations, its affiliate contracts, and its talent and advertising agreements – to Edward J. Noble, owner of the Life Savers Candy Company, for $8 million. It continued to call itself "the Blue Network" until 1945, when it officially became the American Broadcasting Company, a name the company bought from a failed FM radio venture.

Three separate companies, rather than two, now ran the three original radio networks that had been created in the 1920s. But while NBC and CBS were flush with the profits and experience of two decades of radio broadcasting, ABC entered the television era with less of all the things it would take for success: money, technology, government influence, and show business experience.

The ABC television network, launched with a very limited programming schedule and available only in a few large cities, went on the air in 1948. The company remained a step away from bankruptcy for almost a decade and did not reach parity with NBC and CBS until the 1970s. Two things, however, saved it from extinction: (1) a merger with the United Paramount Theaters company (UPT)[8] in 1953, which brought it much-needed cash and show business connections; and (2) several innovative programming collaborations with film studios, something that NBC and CBS had purposely avoided in their effort to keep the moviemakers out of television.

The key figure in the survival of ABC was Leonard Goldenson, the UPT executive who became head of the combined corporation.[9] Though the third great mogul in a group of three, Goldenson, it can be argued, did more in the long run to affect the style and substance of American TV than either of his rivals. While NBC and CBS were putting money and energy into Broadway-style teleplays and vaudeville-like comedy-variety shows, he had no qualms about partnering ABC with Hollywood movie studios to get programming that would make the frail network competitive.

Within a year of joining ABC, Goldenson signed a deal with Walt Disney of Walt Disney Pictures for the first joint venture of a television network and a movie studio. Disney would produce thirty-nine episodes a year of a new hour-long prime-time ABC series to be known as *Disneyland*. A quick success, it reached number 4 in the Nielsen ratings for its first season, making it the highest-rated show to date in the history of the ABC network. At the same time, it was a source of capital and publicity for the new amusement park[10] of the same name that Disney was planning in southern California.

Goldenson's next move, a deal with Warner Brothers Pictures for three hour-long weekly action series, probably did more to kill live television – and assure ABC's salvation – than any other single factor. Movie production was on the wane during the 1950s as television ate away at movie attendance and the number of theaters declined. Double features and "B pictures" were becoming a thing of the past.[11] Stuck with the mammoth new Burbank studio complex that Warner Brothers had built just after the Second World War, studio head Jack Warner made a deal with Goldenson to supply ABC with filmed "action" genre TV series, such as crime shows, Westerns, and war epics. These were a sharp contrast to the talking-heads kitchen dramas that NBC and CBS were presenting on live television. Watching ABC's minuscule audience shares begin to rise in the areas where ABC had station affiliates, Sarnoff and Paley soon followed suit and made similar deals with film houses.

A fourth television network came on line in 1947 as well. The Dumont Network was the brainchild of Allen B. Dumont, an inventor and electronics manufacturer whose cameras and home receivers were considered by many to be technically superior to the more widely sold RCA products. Dumont was personally exasperated by the fact that the profits he was making from his innovations in television technology would be dwarfed by the profits that his arch-rival David Sarnoff would realize from RCA's NBC television network.

Dumont, however, was an individualist competing in a corporate world. He supported his tiny network through the lean years of the freeze with profits from his electronics company, refusing to consider mergers that might have strengthened it in the way that the UPT merger had strengthened ABC. Though a brilliant inventor, he failed to understand the business principle that software (i.e. programming) was at least as essential to success in commercial mass media as hardware, not matter how good that hardware might be.

While ABC had its radio talent contracts to work with it at its inception, the Dumont Network entered the world of showbusiness in its high-tech birthday suit. The network's prime-time schedule consisted in great part of two-hour blocks of pro wrestling and boxing.[12] In 1950, Dumont made a deal with Madison Square Garden to carry, live, any event appearing at the arena. These included such attractions as hockey, basketball, dog shows, the circus, and of course, plenty of wrestling and boxing. NFL football was seen on network television for the first time when Dumont began telecasting Saturday night games in 1953.

Dumont's greatest hit was probably a children's show, *Captain Video and his Video Rangers*, which ran for six years. The network also produced what was arguably the most provocative TV talk show of the era, *Nightbeat*, hosted by Mike Wallace. But Dumont seemed to doom itself even with its successes. Jackie Gleason, who became host of *Dumont Cavalcade of Stars* in 1950, emerged as the first great Dumont star. Within two years, however, CBS chairman William Paley had wooed Gleason away with a far more lucrative contract.

The Dumont Network did not return to the air for the 1955–6 television season. Ironically, more than thirty years later, the old Dumont o&o station group, now owned by the Metromedia Corporation, would be sold to Rupert Murdoch's News Corporation, owner of Twentieth Century Fox. Murdoch made these stations the anchors of the very thing that Allen Dumont had dreamed of – a fourth commercial television network (FOX).

Notes

1 Neither Visa nor MasterCard yet existed. Credit arrangements were made directly between customers and merchants.
2 David Reisman, *The Lonely Crowd* (Garden City, NY: Doubleday, 1953).
3 Tom Wolfe, producer, *The Video McLuhan* (Toronto: McLuhan Productions, 1996). Videotaped program.
4 HUT is an industry acronym for "Household Using TV," or a household that has at least one operating television set.
5 David Adams interviewed by Les Brown, Croton-on-Hudson, New York, December 17, 1996. Audiotape and transcription, Steven H. Scheuer Collection in Television History, Center for the Study of Popular Television, Syracuse University Library. Copyright Syracuse University 1999.
6 "Channel assignment" refers to the grant of exclusive rights to a station to broadcast on a particular frequency or channel in any given radio market. "Transmission power" refers to the wattage or power at which the station broadcasts. If a station has too much power, it may interfere with the signal of other stations. "Bandwidth" refers to the range of channels in which stations may be broadcast and the amount of space each station may take up within that band. In the US, FM radio stations may be assigned channels between 88kHz and 108kHz; AM stations between 540MHz and 1700MHz. Standard radios are manufactured accordingly.
7 Franklin D. Roosevelt's general approach of restructuring the American economy to help bring it back from the Great Depression was known as the "New Deal."
8 United Paramount Theaters should not be confused with Paramount Pictures, the movie studio. Though originally owned by Paramount Pictures, the company was divested following an anti-trust suit in 1949 and it was an independent entity when it merged with ABC in 1953.
9 For a biographical sketch of Leonard Goldenson, including his extraordinary strategy that saved ABC as the third American television network, see David Marc's entry on Goldenson in *Oxford's American National Biography Online* www.anb.org.
10 The term "theme park" did not yet exist.
11 The term "double feature" refers to a movie theater offering two films on the same program for the price of a single admission ticket. The less important (usually the less expense to make) picture was known as the "B picture," and was shown before the main feature.

12 Pro wrestling, though a prominent feature of early television schedules, was not nearly as profitable it would become in the twenty-first century. See Tim Brooks and Earle Marsh, *The Complete Directory to Prime Time Network and Cable TV Shows, 1946 to Present*, 7th edn (New York: Ballantine Books, 1999), for program schedules for 1947–55, which illustrate Dumont's heavy dependence on boxing and wrestling.

~ 5 ~
CORRUPTION AND PLATEAU

By the end of the 1950s the industrial and cultural development of the American broadcast television system had reached a plateau under the oligarchic control of NBC, CBS and ABC.

Technology

The widescale introduction of color was perhaps the only noteworthy TV innovation of the 1960s. As first-generation black-and-white sets went the way of all consumer objects, they were replaced by color sets (often two or more per home). RCA had begun showcasing selected color programs on NBC during the 1950s, and the peacock symbol it used to indicate color programming had grown into the network logo. By 1965, CBS and ABC had joined NBC in committing themselves to "all-color" schedules.[1] Some black-and-white shows that would have likely continued, such as *The Dick Van Dyke Show* (CBS, 1961–5), chose cancellation over retooling for color production, based on economic considerations. Other shows, including TV's most popular show, *The Beverly Hillbillies* (CBS, 1963–71), switched to color production mid-series to remain on the air. But color aside, a serene dullness prevailed.

Despite the stereo capability of its FM sound system, television remained monaural, somehow resisting the national boom in consumer stereo equipment. Sets, even expensive ones, normally came equipped with tiny monaural speakers, and all but the most advanced models lacked auxiliary ports for connection to home component systems. Stereo FM radio improved throughout the 1960s, fueling an enormous boom in the American music industry. But fans knew that, while it might be interesting to *see* Elvis Presley, the Beatles, or the Mamas and the Papas on TV, the music would sound nothing like it did on records or even on a decent radio.

The situation in channel choices also remained status quo. The All-Channel Receiver Bill was passed by Congress, and took effect in 1962. It mandated that all television sets sold in the US be capable of receiving all eighty-one VHF and UHF channels, thus belatedly ending RCA's years of overt and covert attempts to suppress the UHF band for the purpose of maintaining channel scarcity (see chapter 4). Programming choices for almost all viewers remained exactly the same for two decades. The familiar menu, chiseled stonily in *TV Guide*, consisted of a trio of generically similar programs in any given time slot, one each on the local CBS, NBC, and ABC stations. In cities large enough to have independent stations, viewers were offered the further choice of reruns of shows that had been produced for, and cancelled by, the same three networks.

Non-commercial television, then saddled with the unfortunate name "educational TV," was an exotic video oddity limited to those cities large or wise enough to support it. As frightening as it may sound to twenty-first-century ears, it was impossible in most places in the United States to watch any television at all during the hours of 2 a.m. to 5 a.m.! Many people just slept.

Industry

The old radio broadcasting companies, having succeeded in making television a seamless expansion of their existing radio businesses – to the exclusion of all other comers – enjoyed the power and profits appropriate to a cartel. The movie studios, bouncing around between bankruptcy courts and corporate raider/white knight fiscal scenarios, could no longer afford to see television as an enemy or even a rival. Instead the film industry embarked on a path of long-term economic cooperation. Ultimately the studios, as well as the networks, record companies, book publishers, et al., would all wind up as sibling divisions in a handful of media conglomerates.

Art

The "movies" (in the sense, that is, of dating, eating popcorn, and sitting in a dark room with an audience of strangers) remained a vital social phenomenon and continued to play a crucial role in the national courtship ritual by providing a default location for teenagers needing a place to make out, as well as for viewers of all ages feeling "the urge to get out of the house for a change." The "cinema" (in the sense, that is, of *auteur* directors, college film courses, and the ineffable elegance of light flickering at twenty-four frames per second) endured, if just barely, as an intellectual ideal and an aesthetic keepsake. As homes and individuals were outfitted with a widening array of media capabilities over the next two decades, film, as experienced by most Americans, lost its identity as a distinct artistic form, mutating into a type of content or software for other media hardware, such as VCRs, laser disk players, airplane cabins, and DVDs.

This transformation of film from a singular medium, which produced its own art form, to a content genre made for play on other media, began ironically enough with the decision of the networks to abandon live prime-time telecasts in favor of what was then called the "telefilm." In 1953, 80 percent of network television had been broadcast live. By 1960 this figure had declined to 36 percent – and much of that was news or sports. The live anthology dramas, which by necessity had depended on the playwright's ancient craft of creating dramatic tension from the intellectual and emotional energies of words, were canceled, one by one. The filmed series that replaced them, in all but a very few cases, dropped the "heavy stuff" and won their audiences with outdoor shooting and action, which allowed for chase sequences, shoot-outs, and other depictions of physical violence.

In both fact and spirit TV drama was relocated from the New York stage to the Los Angeles soundstage. While the network brass chose to remain close by their Madison Avenue customers and Wall Street bankers, they were quick to see the advantages of shipping out program production to Hollywood, a place that seemed far away from what Robert Sarnoff, the heir-apparent at NBC, had called "depressing Beatnik influences."[2]

One of the notable cultural effects of the new prominence of "action-adventure" telefilm series was the spectacular rise of the TV Western series. Since the country's startup, stories set on the frontier had been a staple of American popular culture, finding their way into magazines, novels, movies, radio, comic books, and other narrative media. Network interest, beginning with the ABC–Warner Brothers agreement in 1955 (see chapter 4), opened up prime time as a territory ripe for settlement.

The movie studios, owning warehouses full of period costumes and sets, as well as having contracts and contacts with appropriately experienced directors and writers, and even their own horse farms, were singularly prepared to meet the furious pace of television production. At the close of the 1958–9 season, the four highest-rated shows on TV (and seven of the Nielsen Top Ten) were horse operas. Not surprisingly, a whopping thirty Westerns were offered up the following year.

In comedy, stage yielded to screen as well. The live, vaudeville-style entertainment of such pioneer stars as Milton Berle, Sid Caesar, and Jack Carter disappeared from television more gradually than live drama, but no less certainly. The creativity of some of the early TV clowns, especially Caesar, had impressed critics, while their television adaptations of old-school banana-peel slapstick had won them high ratings. Some of the comedy-variety stars, notably Jackie Gleason and Red Skelton, would remain on prime-time TV for decades, playing to their aging audiences. But, with the coming of the telefilm, the comedy genre of network choice became the sitcom.

As early as 1951, *I Love Lucy* had demonstrated the money-making potential of a filmed sitcom by leaping over a field dominated by live comedy-variety shows to become number 1 in the ratings. Yet there was little in the content of *I Love Lucy* that was "cinematic" per se. In fact, if it were not for the unwavering desire of Lucille Ball and Desi Arnaz to raise a family in Los Angeles, the same show could have easily been done live from New York, as was otherwise the norm.

Some filmed sitcoms did make use of cinematic special effects. These included *The People's Choice* (a talking dog), *Mr. Ed* (a talking horse), *My Mother, the Car* (a talking automobile), and *My Favorite Martian* (levitation, and other alien hocus-pocus). This developed into a steady subgenre of situation comedy that eventually yielded such hits as *Bewitched*, *I Dream of Jeannie*, and *Sabrina the Teenage Witch*.

But camera tricks were less important in the decision to shift from live comedy-variety shows to filmed sitcoms than the two great industrial advantages of situation comedy: (1) pilots and episodes could be shown to test audiences and focus groups whose reactions could be recorded and measured, something near and dear to the hearts of the advertising agencies who were billing their clients with ever-increasing fees for TV commercials; (2) producers of filmed series could resell their shows to local stations and foreign distributors, following their network production runs. Sitcoms have dominated the syndicated rerun market ever since.

Changes in the character of the TV audience went hand in hand with the conversion to film production. In the introductory years of television (circa 1947–52), stations only existed in the largest cities and sets were quite expensive. The typical TV viewer of the early period was wealthier, better educated, and tended to be more urbane than the average American. Mindful of this, the commercial networks actually aired adaptations of plays by Shakespeare, Ibsen, and Shaw (though there was no shortage of wrestling, boxing, or roller derby either).

But the television explosion that followed the end of the freeze (see chapter 4) ended all that. Hundreds of new stations came on line, each adding hundreds of thousands of new viewers to the potential audience for a given show. With masses to sell to, true mass production of sets became possible. The falling price of TV sets turned what had been an expensive toy of the rich into the entertainment bargain of the century. In 1950, only 9 percent of American households had television; by 1959, that had grown to 85.9 percent. Virtual saturation of more than 98 percent was reached by 1962.

With so few channels available, audiences could number in the tens of millions for even "third-place" shows. A solid hit would draw 30 million or more weekly viewers. With advertising rates rising proportionately, whatever idealism there had been in the industry about "quality programming" or "public service" became a sentimental legacy of the days when the tastes of the educated classes needed to be catered to. Though the phrase did not yet exist, the age of "least objectionable programming" had begun.

Least objectionable programming

Least objectionable programming (LOP) is a term usually credited to Paul Klein, who headed NBC programming during the 1970s. However, the practice preceded the term. The LOP theory maintained that in a television menu consisting of only three networks, all offering generically and stylistically similar programs, a viewer was likely to watch a show not because he or she had some particular enthusiasm for it, but rather out of the belief that the chosen program was least likely to contain things that he or she disliked. Otherwise put, a lack of objectionable material was more crucial to the success of a program than the presence of any attractions it might have.

In attempting to capture the largest share of a massive viewing audience from two competitors, there was no percentage in trying to attract any particular segment of the audience (young, old, male, female, etc.) because the very things that might attract one segment of the audience might cause a greater total number of viewers to tune out. The prominence of the LOP theory during the 1960s among network executives had the result of making TV an extremely bland medium, emphatically devoid of social, intellectual, or artistic issues or contexts.[1] The LOP theory became obsolete in the mid-1980s, as the proliferation of new cable channels opened up the American TV market to demographically targeted programming.

1 There were a few exceptions to this rule. The most compelling of these is *The Defenders* (CBS, 1961–5), a courtroom drama that was produced on film in New York and written by Reginald Rose and other veterans of the live anthology drama programs.

Scandals and Shake-Outs

In 1959, two events underlined the changes that were shaping the television industry and reshaping American culture. The first was the quiz show scandal. Beginning with the success of *The $64,000 Question* in 1955, live prime-time network quiz shows, offering large cash prizes, emerged as a wildly popular form of prime-time programming. In the fall of 1956, there were fifteen such series airing on the three networks each week, with six of them among the thirty highest-rated shows of the season. As the boom continued over the next two years, however, allegations began circulating that some of these shows were frauds; that popular contestants were being given answers to questions in advance, while unpopular contestants were being eliminated with especially difficult questions, or even bribed to give wrong answers. However, public trust in the broadcasting trust was so great at this time that when a guilty former contestant, Herbert Stempel, offered his eyewitness account to several New York newspapers, they dismissed his story at first.[3] It took a Congressional investigation to convince the public that they were being lied to by TV.

While in all likelihood many or most viewers were simply annoyed by the sudden cancellation of some of their favorite quiz shows, there were, in the minds of others, good reasons for public outrage. The same three companies that had become the principal providers and distributors of public information in the US were broadcasting gross acts of public deception on a daily basis, and they continued to do so until they were caught. Was this purposeful blurring of the line between fact and fiction limited to the quiz shows? If ever there was a time for the federal government to exercise the legal power over broadcasting it had asserted since the earliest days of radio, this was it. Would licenses be revoked? Would moguls go to jail? Would enormous fines be levied against multi-billion-dollar companies who had sworn their duty to the public trust as FCC license-holders?

None of the above. Despite the fact that they had profited immensely from the popularity of the phony quiz shows that they had been presenting to the public for years, the networks immediately divorced themselves from responsibility, blaming everything on the individual producers of the programs, in whom they had "foolishly" placed their confidence. These producers, who were guilty as blamed, indeed suffered the personal humiliation of getting caught. But not much else. All avoided jail or financial penalty (beyond that caused by the cancellation of their shows). After hiatuses long enough to satisfy the shrinking national attention span, some even went back into TV game show production. The team of Dan Enright and Jack Barry, who had produced *Twenty-One*, the most spectacularly fraudulent (and popular) game show of them all, produced several daytime game show hits in the 1970s, including *The Joker Is Wild* (syndicated, 1976–91). They even spun off a children's version of *Joker* for Saturday mornings. Only the big-money prime-time quiz show genre itself was punished. After forty years of exile from prime time, ABC deemed the prisoner rehabilitated in the cable era and paroled it with *Who Wants To Be A Millionaire?* in 1999.

Individual contestants did not fare quite as well. Charles Van Doren, the most adored and well-known of the quiz show winners, is a case in point. A Columbia University English instructor and a member of a family of famous writers and scholars, Van Doren must be counted among the first manufactured "media personalities" of the emerging Information Age. In the wake of his appearances on *Twenty-One*, he appeared on the cover of *Time* magazine and was even hired by NBC to co-host the *Today Show*.

When the scandal broke, Van Doren at first denied any involvement. On November 2, 1959, however, after being subpoenaed by Congress, he confessed that he had in fact been given answers to questions in advance. Not only did Van Doren lose the fruits of his celebrity status, but he was immediately fired by Columbia University, thus ending his Ivy League career. Today, of course, any number of schools might have snatched him up for the free press ("We are a diverse institution that is dedicated to the principle that every person deserves a second chance, among others"). But, times being what they were, Van Doren hid himself from the public eye and worked as a writer and editor in relative obscurity for the rest of his life. Van Doren, of course, had tried to keep up the lie. Things went worse for Herbert Stempel, the whistle-blower who first brought the story to public attention; he ended up working for the New York City Transit Authority in full obscurity.

The second big negative of the turn of the decade was the attention given to one of the season's new shows, *The Untouchables*, an ABC crime drama set in prohibition-era Chicago. The series was scorned by the reviewers of the day for what they saw as excessive violence and implied ethnic slurs against Italian Americans. Later generations of post-*Godfather* critics, conditioned to seeing more violence portrayed much more graphically, have since rehabilitated the show as a kind of TV mutant of gangster *film noir*.

The frequent machine-gun battles and pre-Miranda speakeasy raids that characterized *The Untouchables*, especially when considered in the context of the Westerns and other action series that were pervading prime time, contributed to a growing perception that television programming was becoming too violent. This was television's entry into the "public outcry over what the media are doing to our children" drama that either had or would surround such pop-cult phenomena as detective novels, gangster movies, comic books, rap music, and computer games. Cultural watchdogs, both divine and agnostic, demanded that "something be done."

As public "outrage" with violence continued to find its way into the mass media, *The Untouchables* (ABC, 1960–3) emerged as a logical rallying point. Not only did each episode contain multiple incidents of shootings, stabbings, stranglings, and the like, but the show's chief criminal mastermind, Frank Niti, was a series regular and thus protected from appropriate fatal retribution. It was 1960 and here was a TV show entering the homes of American families that could not even have passed the morality codes designed for theatrical films in the 1930s.

Like vaudeville, the movies, rock 'n' roll, and virtually all the cultural favorites that American youth had passionately embraced before it, TV was perceived by the middle-aged as a threat to the moral fiber of the pubescent. Arguments against television violence that were first rehearsed in Congress in during the late 1950s and early 1960s have not yet fallen into disuse. In some cases defense lawyers have recited them at murder trials.

The short but pithy rebuttal of the television industry to these charges remains as consistent as the charges themselves: "Don't worry. The US Constitution, which I'm sure you love as much as we do, clearly gives us the right to present this material, and there's nothing you can do about it. However, we're gonna do something ourselves about this whole violence business – just wait and see."

Other incidents in the late 1950s, not directly involving the networks or their entertainment programs, also helped destroy the once incontrovertible credibility of the broadcasting cartel. In two separate cases, FCC commissioners were exposed accepting bribes from businessmen whose licenses they were charged with reviewing. As was the case with the quiz show scandals, the naughty were just "sent home" and no one did any jail time.[4]

Even the radio side of the business managed to contribute to negative publicity. Disk jockeys, many of whom had developed elaborate on-air personas, were important gatekeepers in the pop music world of the 1950s. They were able to make or break records and singing groups by giving – or not giving – them air time. Some of the most influential, it turned out, were taking bribes, known as "payola," from record companies in return for repeated play and positive buzz. The payola investigation led to the uncovering of a related over-the-air deception known as "plugola." This was the practice of inserting paid product plugs into radio chatter as if they were innocent personal comments. Successful disk jockeys had huge public followings in the 1950s, especially among teenagers. Payola meant a deejay might be chatting up a particular record because he was bribed to do so. Plugola meant anything a deejay said, even a remark like "Anybody gotta Coke?" might actually be a commercial.[5]

These scandals may seem quaint today, given the greater public acceptance of all mass media as commercial artifice. Since most radio stations abandoned the practice of developing "radio personality" disk jockeys in favor of subscribing to playlists issued to them by corporate services, payola is a moot point. It's hard to imagine any music being played on a commercial radio station today that is not on the air as a result of concerns having little to do with the art of music. "Product placement," as plugola is called today, can be found not only in radio, but also in TV, movies, computer games, and hamburgers. The moral codes of 1959, however, were primitive compared to those of the Information Age, and many people actually thought these things were wrong.

Though it is hardly remembered or even believed any more, television had been greeted by a certain amount of idealism when it first came out of the lab. Intellectuals and partisans of the arts had been encouraged by the appearance of some highly regarded dramatic teleplays and comic performances during the first wave of programming. Violent formulaic action series and low-brainer sitcoms put an end to that. There had been hope among the civic-minded that the democratic

The U-2 incident

Another loss-of-innocence incident that took place after 1959 only tangentially involved television, but in retrospect seems to have foreshadowed things to come. On May 1, 1960, a US air force U-2 spy plane was shot down over the Soviet Union, and its pilot, Captain Francis Gary Powers, was taken prisoner. President Dwight Eisenhower, a leader who symbolized the unity the nation had demonstrated in its Second World War victories, explained that the plane was gathering weather information and had strayed into Soviet air space. It was soon revealed, however, that U-2s regularly engaged in spy activity. Viewers found themselves a long way down the Information Highway from the fireside radio chats of Franklin Roosevelt. Vietnam was right around the corner.

process could be significantly enhanced by massive "town meetings of the air," in which political leaders and candidates could talk directly to the people. Instead, political discourse steadily declined into a bland cacophony of shrinking sound bites and photo ops. The potential for educational and children's programming had seemed limitless. By 1960, it was clear that educational television was being relegated to a handful of underfunded and underpowered stations. Moreover, commercial TV seemed to be revealing itself as a threat to both the education and the moral development of children.

The level of faith in television's possibilities even extended to a belief that it could somehow avoid America's most intractable social problem, racial discrimination. *Ebony*, an African American magazine, predicted in a 1950 article that television would be "free of the racial barriers," which had characterized all previous mass media. At first, the prediction seemed to be coming true. When, *Amos 'n' Andy*, an old radio show full of old racial stereotypes, was brought to TV, the NAACP (National Association for the Advancement of Colored People) led a successful fight to have it cancelled in 1953. But it was replaced by . . . nothing. African Americans had virtually disappeared from prime-time television by 1960.

It is not surprising that a tendency gained the high ground among the nation's educational and intellectual establishments, and among political activists of all stripes, to blame television for everything from the declining performance of children in school to the criminal acts of individuals. Most people, however, just kept watching.

Notes

1 The one exception to the "all-color" rule was CBS's annual presentation of the 1939 film, *The Wizard of Oz*. The film's opening and closing black-and-white sequences were the only black and white moments still broadcast on network television for many years.

2 William Boddy, *Fifties Television: The Industry and its Critics* (Urbana: University of Illinois Press, 1990).

3 See the documentary film *The Quiz Show Scandal* produced by Julian Krainin (PBS Video, 1992). Also see the dramatic feature film *Quiz Show* (1994) directed by Robert Redford, which explores several human dimensions of the scandal.

4 For accounts of the FCC bribery scandals, see Erik Barnouw, *Tube of Plenty* (New York: Oxford University Press, 1996), pp. 199–201.

5 The words "payola" and "plugola" derive from a now obscure root in the history of recorded music. Dating back to the start of the twentieth century, the "Victrola," a phonograph (or wax record player) made by the Victor Company (later RCA Victor) was so popular that Victrola became a synonym for phonograph.

~ 6 ~

DULL AS PAINT AND
JUST AS COLORFUL

TV Rules

By 1960 TV use had soared to some five daily hours per household, and all other mass media had to redefine themselves to fit the new communications regime.[1] Household radio usage had shrunk to below two hours per day. However, two factors insured its place in the new media mix: (1) spiraling automobile use isolated viewers from their TV sets for hours at a time to the benefit of their car radios, and (2) the vastly superior variety and transmission quality of radio made it central to the increasingly segmented American music market.[2]

Meanwhile, at the movie theaters, mostly downtown single screens built during the talking picture boom of the 1930s, weekly attendance plunged from 44 million in 1955 to 17.5 million just five years later.[3] Newsreels, Saturday action serials, cartoons, travelogues, B-pictures and other forms of non-feature cinema went drifting toward nostalgic memory. Theater owners promoted air-conditioning as a selling point for a night out at the movies, hanging giant banners from their marquees declaring, "Come on in. It's COOOOOOL Inside." Meanwhile, RCA, General Electric, Westinghouse, and other TV manufacturers were hard at work building affordable home units. By the end of the decade the studios would be churning out "made-for-television" movies.

Daily newspapers, once considered an essential pillar of American democracy, were dropping like railroads in the path of an Interstate Highway project. Most cities would soon be left with either a single daily, or with morning and evening papers under the editorial control of a single publisher. Weekly magazines, such as *Life* and *Look*, whose photographic portraits of American culture had made them national institutions, no longer seemed to appeal to a public that had already "seen" events on TV. *The Saturday Evening Post* proved no match for *Father Knows Best*.

With entertainment supremacy already firmly within in its grasp, and mass information domination on the horizon, television began to exercise its influence in a wider variety of cultural activities. Politics was among them. On September 26, 1960, a debate between the two major-party candidates for President of the United States was broadcast to the nation, something that had never been done during the radio era. All three existing national networks, CBS, NBC, and ABC, carried the event live – and without commercials – on both their television and radio networks. For the vast majority of viewers that Monday night, including both voters and non-voters, pickings were even slimmer than usual: it was going to be a debate between Richard M. Nixon and John F. Kennedy – or no TV at all. Needless to say the audience was huge. Estimated at 75 million, it set a record to date. A total of four debates were held during the 1960 campaign.

Howard K. Smith Remembers the Nixon–Kennedy Debates

Howard K. Smith was a leading broadcast newsman for half a century. As a CBS radio reporter, he had been stationed in Berlin up to the day the US declared war on Germany. In the television era, he served as anchor of ABC's daily evening news program. Still with CBS in 1960, he was picked by the network to moderate the first of the four debates. He recalled the experience in a 1997 interview:

"It was a series of promotional messages; it wasn't much of a debate. Still, I think it was useful to get them facing one another. They were talking *to* each other. I listened and I kept a little point score. I forget how I did it, but Nixon came out ahead. He was a better debater. That's all there is to it. He could take points and make them better. But then I went back and saw the tape, and it was clear that Kennedy had swept it. A handsome man full of enthusiasm, he had nothing to lose. He was not a famous man then. Nixon was. Nixon had been on television a lot. This was a wonderful opportunity for Kennedy. Nixon looked defeated. 'I should never have agreed to this,' I can imagine him saying to himself. 'The public know me; they don't know him. Now, in one night, I've elevated him to my level.' Nixon was rather defeatist in demeanor and Kennedy was triumphant in demeanor. That registered."

Howard K. Smith, interviewed by David Marc at his home in Bethesda, Maryland, December 8, 1997. Audiotape and transcription, Steven H. Scheuer Collection in Television History, Center for the Study of Popular Television, Syracuse University Library. Copyright Syracuse University 1999.

6.1 SIDEBAR

The Nixon–Kennedy Debates seemed to demonstrate two things in 1960, both of which have since been called into question: (1) television would play a formidable and positive role in helping to realize American democratic ideals of public accessibility to information and participation in political life; (2) the American public-cumaudience had an interest in electoral politics that would be cultivated and served by TV.

A replay of the elegantly grainy black-and-white tapes of the Kennedy–Nixon show reveals a kind of quaint level of video political discourse that was canceled by the networks long ago. Each candidate is given opportunities to speak for whole minutes at a stretch on a single subject. At times the production is almost oblivious to the Incredible Shrinking Attention Span that is now accepted as the imagined target of all televised communication. There seemed to be practical and noble uses for the new medium that might flourish side by side with the industry's bread-and-butter business of selling products (including, of course, these same candidates).

Commercial-free and civic-minded, the Nixon–Kennedy debates gave the networks a cleaner, brighter image than the one that had been created by the recent string of deceit and bribery scandals. In a similar vein, the broadcasting giants began to produce prime-time news documentaries that seemed capable of breaking through to a new level of socially conscious reporting. The main brand names showcasing these hour-long news division pieces were *CBS Reports*, *NBC White Paper*, and *ABC Close-Up*.

Muckraking reporting had long been an honored part of American print journalism. But if radio had done a remarkable job of reporting war news during the 1940s, the news divisions had done little in the way of investigative exposés. TV news, invented and developed by the same executives, continued the general policy of steering clear of controversy.

The notable exception to this almost universal commitment to "objective" reporting was the 1950s prime-time series *See It Now*, which was hosted by broadcast journalism's greatest star, Edward R. Murrow.[4] While virtually all other news and public affairs programs were produced directly by the network news divisions, Murrow and his partner/collaborator Fred W. Friendly formed their own company to produce the show. Having thus limited the liability of CBS for *See It Now* content, Murrow and Friendly were freer to go after controversial subjects and make "editorial" comment. They took every advantage.

In a famous episode of *See It Now*, Murrow dared to voice frank criticism of the tactics used by Senator Joseph McCarthy in his investigations of Communist Party infiltration into such US government agencies as the army and the State Department. There is evidence that McCarthy's downfall, including his eventual censure by the US Senate, began with Murrow's 1953 *See It Now* exposé (though Martin Agronsky had made radio broadcasts critical of McCarthy as early as 1951).[5] Other *See It Now* episodes explored such subjects as the discharge of a US army private

SIG MICKELSON

Sig Mickelson was in charge of CBS television news, beginning in 1951, when it was just an offshoot of the network's radio news operations. He became the first president of CBS News in 1964. Here he relates how he chose to introduce a new technology into programming.

"AMPEX was first with videotape. They took a unit to Chicago to demonstrate it to the CBS affiliates in April of 1956 and that was the first demonstration anywhere in the world of videotape. RCA, which owned NBC, was their competitor, so AMPEX wanted CBS to use it. We [CBS News] had a tape unit available by the end of 1956, but we weren't sure just how we'd use it. It was rather cumbersome, a big two-inch quad-head unit. So I got an idea and I said to Bill McPhail, the director of sports, 'Look, we're doing the Kentucky Derby live next week. Why don't you go to the technical operations staff and get them to record the Kentucky Derby and then just turn it around and play it back again.' He called me back and said, 'They say it's too risky. They won't do it.' I said, 'Well, tell 'em to go ahead, anyway.' So they did it – and it worked. Millions were watching, but nobody could figure out how in the world we did it. It wasn't instant replay in the sense you think of it today, but it was the first use of videotape on the air and the ancestor of a much more sophisticated style."

Sig Mickelson was interviewed by David Marc, San Diego, September 6, 1996. Videotape and transcription, Steven H. Scheuer Collection in Television History, Center for the Study of Popular Television, Syracuse University Library. Copyright Syracuse University 1999. The picture of Mickelson is from a second interview, videotaped and transcribed, which is also part of the Scheuer Collection.

because of his father's left-wing politics and the first-ever television report on the relationship between tobacco and lung cancer.

In 1955, *See It Now* lost its regular half-hour prime-time spot and was reduced to occasional special presentations. In 1958, with quiz show popularity spiking, it disappeared completely. However, the scandals had given CBS chairman William Paley second thoughts about the value that public-spirited journalism might bring to the company. *CBS Reports*, which premiered in 1959, was to be the network's showcase for hard-hitting documentaries. It was not conceived as a vehicle for a "news star" – Paley had perhaps had his fill of that. Instead, it was hosted by a rotating group of some of the network's most highly respected correspondents, many of whom had been household names since their radio reporting during the Second World War.[6]

Murrow and Friendly dived right in to the opportunity presented by *CBS Reports* with "Harvest of Shame," an exposé of the economic and social conditions under which American migrant farmworkers and their families were living. The squalor and the indignities faced by these "forgotten" workers were a shocking contrast to the rah-rah boom-time imagery of post-war America that had become the atmosphering principle of commercial TV.

The hour-long black-and-white piece follows a group of farmworkers through their yearly work cycle, from their winter quarters in Florida and as they move up the eastern seaboard into the fields and orchards of the northeast harvests. A variety of speakers are interviewed. The US Secretary of Labor expresses sympathy with the plight of the workers. A picker talks about the difficulties of affording milk for her children. A planter explains that the farmworkers are satisfied by a simpler life. A New Jersey schoolteacher who works with the migrating children for a few months each year explains how circumstances make it virtually impossible for them to get even a rudimentary education. The fact that this teacher is an African American woman was itself a didactic flourish at a time when the few non-whites who appeared on TV were inarticulate, if not downright buffoons.

Staunch political liberals, Murrow and Friendly made the case to the American public for reforms of federal labor laws to help alleviate the farmworkers' plight. However, while "Harvest of Shame" raised public consciousness of the issue, it failed to provoke any legislation. Substantial reform would only take place after more than a decade of union organizing and farm product boycotts led by Cesar Chavez of the United Farmworkers Union.

Another *CBS Reports* episode did provoke immediate legislative action. "The Silent Spring of Rachel Carson," hosted by Charles Collingwood, was based on Carson's controversial book *Silent Spring*, concerning the health dangers posed by agricultural pesticides, especially DDT.[7] Its presentation on national television was an early milestone in creating public awareness of the ecological dangers posed to a society that had so thoroughly cast its lot with unbridled technology. The show helped spread the alarm of a small group of activists and experts into a grassroots campaign culminating in the federal banning of DDT. "The Silent Spring" demonstrated that television could be a force in galvanizing public opinion in other areas than product consumption.

But this was not the kind of power that the broadcasting companies had in mind for TV. The price of a commercial spot was increasing year to year, and it soon became apparent to the networks that this type of content was irreconcilably incompatible with the overpowering commercial potentials of the medium. Network news documentaries gradually redistributed the weight of their subject matter in favor of "informational," "historical," and "human interest" stories. The commercial 60-minute investigative form suffered a deathblow from the success of a prime-time news show titled, ironically, *60 Minutes*. Here in-depth, one-hour investigative reporting was shattered into three or four shorter pieces.

Two obvious factors doomed muckraking documentaries on commercial television: (1) they did not do as well in the ratings as sitcoms, cop shows, or any other known form of American entertainment television; and (2) insults to advertisers or unwelcome investigations of their actions are an unavoidable cost of engaging in the business of investigative journalism. Murrow, the great exponent of the form, understood this. Disenchanted by the commercial juggernaut of television, and especially hurt by the impact this was having on the CBS News operation he had helped to build, Murrow resigned in 1961 to accept President Kennedy's offer of the directorship of the US Information Agency. A furious chain-smoker since childhood, he died soon after of lung cancer.

Also joining the Kennedy administration in 1961 was a young Chicago lawyer named Newton Minow, whom the president had appointed as Chair of the Federal

Edward R. Murrow (April 25, 1908–April 27, 1965)

Born in Polecat Creek, North Carolina, Ed Murrow grew up in Skagit Valley, Washington. He majored in speech at Washington State University and was elected president of the National Student Federation in 1929. In 1935 he joined the Columbia Broadcasting System (CBS) as Director of Talks and Education. That year he was sent to Europe by CBS to arrange for cultural broadcast exchanges with European radio networks. Though he had no experience as a journalist or radio broadcaster, he was so alarmed by what he saw in Nazi Germany that he got permission to broadcast news and news events. Murrow made no secret of his sympathies when on the air, developing an advocacy style that is rare in commercial network broadcasting. As it became clear that the world was heading toward war, CBS chairman William Paley gave Murrow the resources to build a news team. Under Murrow's leadership, CBS News emerged as the premier American broadcaster of world war. "I hire reporters," he said, "not announcers." After the war, Murrow adapted his advocacy style for television. But TV profits were not compatible with ruffling feathers and Murrow was nudged out of power at CBS.

6.2
SIDEBAR

Communications Commission. Unlike the largely ceremonial post offered to Murrow, Minow's position, at least theoretically, held power that could revolutionize the direction of the mushrooming TV industry of the 1960s.

Under US law the airwaves belong to the public, and the FCC is the regulatory agency that oversees their use in the public interest. Every broadcast station in the US must be licensed by the FCC, which, in turn, has the power to rescind or to decline to renew that license where it finds good cause. The free speech provisions of the Bill of Rights prevent the FCC from exercising prior restraint or censorship over television content, but the agency is charged with the duty of evaluating whether or not individual television and radio stations are operating within the "public interest, convenience, and necessity." Though the FCC has exercised its power to revoke licenses only a very few times, it is legally capable of putting an American broadcaster out of business.

Before the deregulatory actions of the 1980s freed station owners of any real responsibility to serve the public interest, this power was regarded seriously by the industry. For the national television networks, FCC licensing powers presented two kinds of threat. If one of a network's affiliates failed to win license renewal, network service to that market could be disrupted and audience size (and commercial profits) diminished. But, more importantly to the networks, they are themselves the owners and operators of stations in the most lucrative markets, and these "o&o's" have traditionally been their most profitable properties.

So, when the National Association of Broadcasters (NAB) invited Newton Minow to speak at its annual convention on May 9, 1961, the members were anxious to hear what the Kennedy administration's new and relatively unknown FCC Chair had to say. Based on past experience with most FCC commissioners, they generally expected to be congratulated for the fine job they were doing, reminded of broadcasting's public mission, and go on with business as usual.

Indeed Minow began his speech by praising the industry. He lauded the "golden-age" anthology dramas (which the networks had all but purged from their schedules); he lauded their hard-hitting documentary series (which the networks already knew to be money-losers and regarded as an obligatory pain in the neck); and he lauded the presidential debates (which helped put John Kennedy, and therefore Minow, in office). He even went so far as to say, "when television is good . . . nothing is better."

The station owners would have happily retired to the reception area if the speech had ended there. However, it did not. Instead Minow launched into an articulation of what many American intellectuals and educators were thinking – and in some cases still are thinking – about TV. "When television is bad," he continued, "nothing is worse." He invited the owners to watch their stations from sign-on to sign-off, and he assured them that what they would see would be "a vast wasteland" of "game shows, violence, audience participation shows, formula comedies about totally unbelievable families, blood and thunder, mayhem, violence, sadism, murder, western bad men, western good men, private eyes, gangsters, more violence, and cartoons," all punctuated by an endless stream of commercials.

Minow's language grew powerful and aggressive to a degree far beyond anything the industry had previously heard from the US government. "I understand that many people feel that in the past licenses were often renewed *pro forma*. I say to you now: renewal will not be *pro forma* in the future. There is nothing permanent or sacred about a broadcast license."

The speech caused an uproar among the captains of communication. As still happens when they are publicly criticized for the programs they air, network and station executives headed straight for the shelter of the First Amendment, claiming that neither the government nor any one else could interfere with their rights as Americans to express themselves by airing any programs they wanted, no matter how banal or violent or mind-numbing they might be.

CBS, which at this point utterly dominated television entertainment in ratings, profits, and prestige, hedged its bets by taking the high road. The network sped up development of several prestigious new drama series that focused on topical social issues. The most successful of these – and perhaps the highest achievement in courtroom drama ever to reach prime time – was *The Defenders*. Produced in New York by anthology drama veteran Reginald Rose, and written by a staff of his anthology drama colleagues, *The Defenders* took on such subjects as abortion, racism, and even the political blacklisting practices of the television industry. "We knew we were pushing the envelope," series star E. G. Marshall recalled. "Some stations didn't carry it . . . sponsors pulled out or had to be given big discounts." Some forty years later, with several hundred cable channels showing reruns of reruns of failed series, *The Defenders* is rarely seen. Its earnest liberalism is just too painful for the market to bear.

Though the "vast wasteland" speech may claim some responsibility for giving viewers *The Defenders*, *East Side, West Side*, *The Nurses*, and a few other high-end series, Minow was unable to follow through on the promises (or threats) of his speech. While some elements of the Kennedy administration, notably Attorney General Robert Kennedy, supported a tough stand against the dumbing down of television, President Kennedy was convinced to back off by advisors who reminded him that TV had been crucial to his victory in 1960, and that it would be the window through which the American public would see him make his case for re-election in 1964. If he wished to remain his office, he could not afford to alienate the gatekeepers of the medium – no one could. Newton Minow resigned from the FCC in 1963. Lyndon Johnson, a TV station owner, acceded to the presidency following Kennedy's assassination.

E. G. MARSHALL

E. G. Marshall starred as attorney Lawrence Preston in *The Defenders,* arguably the most socially conscious American television series made during the pre-cable era. Here he discusses an episode made in 1963 in which Preston defends a doctor who performs an abortion, despite the fact that the procedure was illegal, under any circumstance, in all fifty states.

E. G. MARSHALL. We knew we were "pushing the envelope," as they say. Some stations didn't carry it and all the sponsors pulled out of the abortion show, except for a watchband company – it was around graduation time, so they got some pay for it.

STEVEN SCHEUER. What was the reason that was given at the time for the sponsor defection?

EGM. Too controversial.

SS. Did the network [CBS] believe that the American public wasn't ready to hear any kind of discussion about abortion?

EGM. The network let it go on, but the sponsors said, "No, we can't sell our product about abortion." It was probably true.

SS. Why might it have been true? Do you think most people would have said "I won't buy that product," just because of the association with the show?

EGM. Absolutely! They wrote letters in if they didn't like a show. They felt it.

E. G. Marshall was interviewed by Steven H. Scheuer, New York City, October 16, 1997. Videotape and transcription, Steven H. Scheuer Collection in Television History, Center for the Study of Popular Television, Syracuse University Library. Copyright Syracuse University 1999. This was Marshall's last interview before his death several months later.

Just Plain Folks

On October 3, 1960, *The Andy Griffith Show* premiered on CBS.[8] Set in the mythical North Carolina town of Mayberry, the sitcom was an immediate ratings success, spending all its eight seasons in the Nielsen Top Ten, and eventually spawning two hit spin-offs, *Gomer Pyle, USMC* (1964–70) and *Mayberry RFD* (1968–71) for the network. *The Beverly Hillbillies* (1963–71), a show that surpassed *Andy Griffith* in the ratings during most of its production run, was the next rural sitcom mega-hit, and it spun off two more, *Petticoat Junction* (1963–70) and *Green Acres* (1965–72). If ratings are to be believed by historians as much as they are by advertising executives, the rural situation comedy became the most popular of all television genres during the 1960s.

The appeal of the rural comedies was multifold. As was the case with most entertainment programs in the pre-cable period, they seemed to provide a cultural anaesthetic of sorts. By presenting a contemporary world devoid of the race riots, war crimes, and peace demonstrations of the 1960s, they functioned as a kind of passive-aggressive rebuttal to the evening news. Whatever the intentions of *The Andy Griffith Show*'s producers and writers might have been, the racial homogeneity of Sheriff Andy Taylor's Mayberry, North Carolina, is reification of what Ralph Ellison characterized as the "invisible" status of African Americans. At the same time, more urbane viewers seemed to enjoy the relentless implicit and explicit deflations of contemporary middle-class pretension that pervaded the genre. *The Beverly Hillbillies* can be particularly merciless in its slapstick portrayal of bourgeois manners in 1960s Los Angeles.

The humor and spirit of the ruralcoms was by no means new to American culture. The shows are part of a long American tradition of hayseed vs. city slicker humor that includes the "rube" routines of the vaudeville stage, the "L'il Abner" comic strip, and the "Ma and Pa Kettle" movie series, among many others. Royal Tyler's *The Contrast* (1789), the very first comedy written and produced for the American stage, concerns a Berkshire Mountains country boy who strikes it rich and moves to New York. Like the *Hillbillies*' Jed Clampett, his unspoiled moral character more than compensates for whatever he lacks in urban savvy.

In terms of TV history, the success of the genre came at a crucial time in the development of American television programming. With Minow gone from the FCC and a station owner sitting in the White House, the scandals faded into the ancient past of a previous decade. The "vast wasteland" license paranoia that had swept through the industry gave way to a renewed sense of license to seek profits wherever they might be found.

The prime-time programming models offered by such series as *The Defenders* (topical drama) and the original *CBS Reports* (investigative journalism) were discarded from network planning. An initiative for new profit centers in areas traditionally reserved for "public service" was undertaken. Commercial-free Sunday religious programming, produced since the radio era in collaboration with the National Council of Churches, was crowded out by professional football coverage. CBS's NFL ratings spiraled. The rival American Football League was introduced on ABC in 1961, later switching to NBC. Double-headers and longer pre- and post-game shows were introduced.

As a result, *Lamp Unto My Feet, Look Up and Live*, and other long-running religious series which had presented didactic dramas, discussions of social issues, and even original oratorios sung by some of the world's great opera singers, were downsized and eventually canceled. Religious and cultural programming was limited to a dwindling string of "specials." When Pamela Ilott, who had been vice-president for religious and cultural programming at CBS for decades, retired in the mid-1970s, the network simply abolished her position – and her entire department.

Commercial programming aimed at children actually increased during this period, but took a direction that made many educators and parents wish it hadn't. Shows such as *Captain Kangaroo* and *Leonard Bernstein's Young People's Concerts*, which made rigorous efforts to separate program content from the marketplace, became relics of another era. New shows, produced to laterally market toys and float corporate product tie-ins, became standard on Saturday mornings and in other slots frequented by minors. The America of the twenty-first century was beginning to take shape.

Television Gothic

Faced with an indifferent White House, Minow and Minowism faded into an industrial bad memory. The networks forged ahead into the 1965–6 season, exploring new applications in the synthesis of psychological theory and artistic technique. Sitcom debuts that season included *Gidget*, starring Sally Field as the Anti-Lolita, a 15-year-old in swimwear frolicking on a California beach, yet somehow protected from the penetration of the sexual revolution; *I Dream of Jeannie*, starring Barbara Eden as an uncorked 2,000-year-old genie with an unexposed navel in the service of an astronaut whom she addresses as "Master"; and *My Mother the Car* (NBC, 1965–6), a sitcom whose title is without metaphor.

While fantasy has always been a source of artistic content, the sitcom, circa 1965–6, went elsewhere for its *mise-en-scène* as well. For example, it was a very good year for the banalization of history. *F Troop* (ABC), set in a post-Civil War frontier army fort, featured an encyclopedic assortment of Native American stereotypes. *Hogan's Heroes* (CBS) perhaps best exemplified the bizarre new direction TV entertainment was taking. Set in a Nazi prison camp, the show hit the Nielsen Top Ten with its very first episode. Supported by an ensemble cast of bumbling Wehrmacht officers and inept Gestapo agents, the Allied prisoners bear the hell of war with such amenities as "a French chef, a steam room and a barbershop."[9]

Live 1950s television, preserved on grainy black-and-white kinescopes, is only available at rarefied cultural institutions such as the Museum of TV and Radio, the Museum of Modern Art, and the Center for the Study of Popular Television. But the filmed TV series of the 1960s have endured in the reruns to become

Peggy Charren, advocate for the improvement of children's programming

In 1968, alarmed by the direction that children's programming had taken, Peggy Charren founded Action for Children's Television (ACT), a grassroots organization dedicated to setting higher standards for the genre. A Boston area homemaker, Charren became involved in organizing children's book fairs for schools and libraries. Her passionate dedication to articulating parental worries about the violence and inanity of kid-TV eventually led her to become a national spokesperson whose voice was heard in the halls of Congress. In a 1998 interview, she speaks about the formation of ACT.

"We had this incredible coalition of labor unions and health organizations and religious groups and education groups that stood up with us. When you testify in Congress, you have to have standing. I could say, 'We represent 135 million people.' Granted, I would say, some of these people could belong to two organizations and maybe we're double-counting. But 135 million was something you could talk about! So that was sort of fun. We started to make a difference. I didn't think Nixon or Ford or Carter were so terrific, but the FCC actions on children taken by those Commissions was very good. Dick Riley, the FCC Chair under Ford, came out with a policy statement that was really quite strong, although at the time I remember saying, 'What kind of nonsense is this? A policy statement? It should be a rule!' But I've since told Dick Riley that, looking back, it was like the Magna Carta of children's television. There were hearings that continued at the FCC all those years. What started to happen were things like the *After School Specials* at ABC, which were as good as television ever has to get. Hour specials based on very good pre-teen and young-teen books, novels, with the best actors, the best writers. It was like a *Masterpiece Theater* for children. CBS and NBC did a few of those; not as many and for as long as ABC. There were two advertisers: Kelloggs and McDonalds. They bought into that program even though it wasn't quite as good a buy as Saturday morning."

Peggy Charren, interviewed by David Marc, Boston, May 5, 1998. Audiotape and transcription, Steven H. Scheuer Collection in Television History, Center for the Study of Popular Television, Syracuse University Library. Copyright Syracuse University 1999.

6.3 SIDEBAR

fundamental factors in Century-21 USA: the continuing subjects of feature films and stand-up comedy routines, the iconographical models for vitamin lines and toothbrushes and, of course, the continuing topic of viewer conversation. Sexy genies, housewife witches, talking horses, pet dinosaurs, the cast of *Gilligan's Island* . . .

Notes

1   Christopher H. Sterling and John M. Kitross, *Stay Tuned: A Concise History of American Broadcasting* (Belmont, CA: Wadsworth, 1978; 2nd edn, 1990). This statistic refers to the number of hours that a set was believed to be "on" during a given day, rather than the number of hours any particular individual was watching it.

2   Beginning with its arrival in the early 1950s, rock 'n' roll music was viewed by some segments of American society as a corrupting force among youth. In the age of "least objectionability," the TV networks had to tread lightly when they presented it. For example, in 1957 CBS would only allow its cameras to show Elvis Presley above the waist during his appearance on *The Ed Sullivan Show*.

3   Robert Sklar, *Movie-Made America* (New York: Vintage Books, 1994), p. 288.

4   A radio version, *Hear It Now*, had preceded it on CBS in the late 1940s.

5   Agronsky received a Peabody Award for his ABC radio broadcasts against McCarthy in 1951. However, it was a sign of the growing power of television that no big fuss was made until TV took up the matter. See David Marc's entry on Martin Agronsky in *Oxford's American National Biography Online www.anb.org*.

6   The network still uses the title "CBS Reports" for its prime-time news presentations. However these programs bear little resemblance to the muckraking pieces discussed here.

7   Rachel Carson, *Silent Spring* (Boston: Houghton Mifflin, 1962).

8   *The Andy Griffith Show* was not the first rural sitcom to appear on network TV. That distinction goes to *The Real McCoys* (CBS, 1957–63), concerning a West Virginia family that migrates to the San Joaquin Valley of California, which was the first of the genre to reach television.

9   Tim Brooks and Earle Marsh, *The Complete Directory to Prime Time Network and Cable TV Shows, 1946 to Present*, 7th edn (New York: Ballantine Books, 1999), p. 453.

A MYTH IS AS GOOD
AS A SMILE

Having escaped punishment for both the scandals of the 1950s and the programming decisions of the 1960s, the once heavily regulated broadcasting industry began to truly feel its oats in the 1970s. The great experiment in cultural distribution for money that had begun with mass-circulation magazine publishing in London, and accelerated into mass radio broadcasting in New York, had spun out of effective civil control in the television era. The tangle of advertising agencies, market research firms, and media production and distribution companies had grown into something greater than the sum of its parts: a powerful entertainment-industrial complex willing, able, ready, and anxious to commodify any and every aspect of information or imagination that the trafficking would allow.

Despite the rhetoric of legal constraint inherited from the vanishing America of traditionalist conservatives (Herbert Hoover) and activist liberals (Franklin Roosevelt), the airwaves had become, in effect, no more a public property than a General Motors assembly plant or a Silicon Valley software farm. Free at last, the industry boiled down the hodge-podge of early entertainment TV to three dramatic genre products: 30-minute sitcoms based on character identification and language play; 60-minute dramas based on either physical action, emotional distress, or both; and 120-minute commercially segmented films, which were either re-edited theatrical releases or designed from scratch specifically for TV.

All three of the commercial broadcasting networks accepted all three formulas during the 1960s, to the almost complete exclusion of genre experimentation in prime time. However, because of the central position that television now held in the fully penetrated nation, there was an intensification of competition among the triad for the greater profits that even a fraction of a rating point could bring. This led to a degree of experimentation in content. Before examining the new content ideas of the 1970s, it is worth understanding the relative positions of the three networks in the ratings previous to that decade.

Competition in network television had been static since the mid-1950s. CBS sat atop the prime-time ratings year after year, with NBC showing enough profit as runner-up to satisfy RCA, its parent conglomerate. RCA, which had dominated radio technology as well as content, seemed to lose interest in the goose that had been laying its golden eggs. Top management became more interested in diversifying the corporate portfolio than in beefing up NBC television or radio programming. They acquired companies such as Hertz Rent-a-Car and Whirlpool Appliances, and eventually sold off the radio network that had started it all. David Sarnoff, who had never been much interested in the programming side of the business, turned his attention to new technologies, including such potentially explosive sellers as home nuclear reactors.[1] Meanwhile, his rival William Paley, short on patents and long on showmanship, made a point of spending whatever it took to put the stars – including many former NBC radio stars – on CBS television.

Following the demise of DuMont in 1955, ABC took sole possession of the basement for the next twenty years. Stabilized by its merger with United Paramount Theaters, however, the company made slow but sure gains under the leadership of its CEO Leonard Goldenson, adding popular shows to its line-up as well as new affiliated stations to its audience reach. By the early 1970s, three-way ratings races were common in many time periods: during the late 1970s, ABC began to beat NBC in the ratings, and, in 1978–9, full parity was confirmed as the no longer sad sister sprinted past CBS to actually win the season.

No medium could yet compete with broadcast television as a mass commercial communication system, but the broadcasting companies began to undermine the structure of their thirty-year oligopoly by competing more actively with each other. While the total number of viewers was still the figure upon which most money changed hands, the key to winning the ratings race in the newly competitive environment was capturing an extra fraction of the emerging generation of viewers, the 18–34-year-olds. These were the first human beings that had not known life without television. Unlike their parents, so many of whom had stood slack-jawed in front of appliance shop windows watching whatever magical images the happy oracle of the post-war world was wont to deliver, the TV babies had developed a degree of immunity to the endless recyclings of "market-proven" narratives: forgotten-birthday sitcom episodes; least-likely-suspect-is-the-murderer copshows; families-reuniting-around-the-tragedy-of-cancer movies, and as many as half a dozen others. Some preferred to listen to the radio, which had become a vital medium for youth-oriented music, little of which was played on TV for fear of making their parents go crazy. Network programmers and production executives went foraging for ideas outside the box of tricks that had worked so well for them in the past. Gradually it dawned on them that they needed to look no further than their own evening news shows for exciting new fiction.

When No News Was Good News . . . in Prime Time

In the beginning, American television, like radio before it, had a tradition of maintaining a distinct dichotomy between entertainment and non-fiction programming. Stories concerning the Cold War and the civil rights movement, to name the two prominent mega-stories of the early TV period, were dutifully reported on network news programs and occasionally examined in prime-time documentaries. These subjects were, however, steadfastly ignored in the storylines of popular prime-time drama.

The reluctance of the broadcast networks and their corporate sponsors to get involved with "current events" in their entertainment programs was easy to understand. The very suggestion of what are now called "hot button" issues was thought to make people feel anxiety-ridden, even depressed, and these were emotions that sponsors did not want associated with their products. To make matters worse, when such subject matter is presented to audiences numbering in the tens of millions, no matter how tepid the treatment might be, it inevitably gives rise to controversies that produce negative viewer reactions. This was frightening not only to sponsors and networks, but also to a television production community that had been living under the threat of politically motivated blacklisting for most of its existence. As a result, the ignoring of socially important issues in prime-time drama was an internalized "given" that required little overt enforcement.

This unusual cultural dichotomy between a national drama and a national history became painfully apparent during the 1960s. By mid-decade each network was offering a half-hour daily news summary scheduled at dinnertime, which came to be regarded as a kind of mid-tech updating of the vision of the American family discussing the daily newspaper (presumably with Clifton Webb sitting at the head of the table).[2] In addition to these regularly scheduled half-hour reports, the networks often galvanized the nation by abruptly pre-empting episodes of weekly series (yes, actually canceling scheduled, even well-promoted, programming), or by having their news divisions "break in" with on-the-spot coverage of significant breaking events, such as urban riots, presidential assassinations, and acts of war.

The network dinnertime news summaries were of great consequence to the public psyche – and had much higher ratings – before news-free cable choices revealed interest in the temporal world to be little more than a viewing taste; perhaps an exotic viewing taste. Cable undermined daily network news in two ways: on the one hand, "all-news" outlets, such as CNN, MSNBC, and FOX News, had the effect of selecting out news junkies from the general population; at the same time, scores of new cable stations supplied the gen-pop with dozens of appealing choices that did not offer any news at all. When a war is boring, why not watch HBO?

BETSY PALMER

Betsy Palmer appeared in many early television plays, including Paddy Chayevsky's "Marty" (1953), a "classic" of live television. She was a regular panelist for ten years on *I've Got A Secret,* a prime-time weekly game show, during the 1950s and 60s and later played the mother of the infamous hockey-masked mass-murderer Jason in the *Friday the 13ᵗʰ* movies. Here Palmer remembers two of the hundreds of acting careers that were affected by the practice of politically motivated blacklisting in the television industry.

"We had an actor by the name of Will Hare on the *Miss Susan* show. All of a sudden, Will Hare, who worked pretty regularly, could not get himself arrested, as far as being a performer is concerned. It got so bad that he started a restaurant in Westport, Connecticut (which became a big hit and he made stacks and stacks of money). But we never found out what it was until years later when [blacklisting] was all over and done with. The problem was that his name had gotten mixed up with Will Geer's name on one of those anti-Red lists. Now Will Geer never made any bones about *not* being a card-holding member of the [Communist] Party. He later came back as Grandpa on *The Waltons.* But 'Hare' sounds like 'Geer' and they both went by the name of 'Will,' and that's why poor Will Hare couldn't work on TV anymore."

Betsy Palmer was interviewed by David Marc, Beverly Hills, March 13, 1997, and Studio City, California, April 3, 1997. Audiotape and transcription, Steven H. Scheuer Collection in Television History, Center for the Study of Popular Television, Syracuse University Library. Copyright Syracuse University 1999. The picture of Palmer is from a third interview, videotaped and transcribed, which is also part of the Scheuer Collection.

But during the 1960s and 1970s, the daily news shows anchored by Walter Cronkite (CBS), John Chancellor (NBC), and Howard K. Smith (ABC) plastered the screen with pictures of an increasingly violent and threatening world, while prime-time dramaturgy stood its ground in favor of imitations of life lived 1950s lite. The contrast came to its most acute crisis in Vietnam War coverage. The popularity of Lyndon Johnson that led to his landslide presidential victory in 1964 was negated in large part by the daily film footage of battlefield activity, which was complemented by videotape of Pentagon brass gingerly predicting imminent American victory while anti-war demonstrations raged in the streets. Richard Nixon, elected in 1968 on a "peace (with honor)" or, perhaps more accurately, "(peace with) honor" platform, failed to deliver either, extending the run of blood, guts, lies, and demonstrations for six more seasons. Yet somehow, each evening, when the news ended, so did the war and its spin-offs.

In defiance of mainstream Western traditions, television, which by now had become the vessel of American language and drama, offered no prime-time series or even any episodes of dramatic series that dealt with Vietnam. A look at two sitcoms, one that actually mentioned Vietnam and one that did not, illustrates the point. In *Julia* (NBC, 1967–70), starring Diahann Carroll, it is established in the series premiere that the title character's husband died in Vietnam, something the network thought might help gain acceptance for the title character, the first to be played by an African American woman on US TV since the early 1950s. The subject of Vietnam was never brought up again during the show's three-year run. Perhaps the most astounding example of social denial can be found in *Gomer Pyle*,

USMC (CBS, 1964–70). Though set in the putative "present" at a US Marine base in California, never once in any of its 151 episodes is Vietnam mentioned or is there any evidence in the videotext that a war involving half a million American soldiers is underway.

Shows Without Trees

The years 1968 to 1972 constitute a milestone in the decline of the "old television" programming that had been adapted from pre-TV media. Shows rooted aesthetically, and in some cases chronologically, in the 1940s and 1950s, including *Ed Sullivan*, *Lawrence Welk*, *Gunsmoke*, *Red Skelton*, *Jackie Gleason*, and other long-enduring hits, were summarily axed, without regard for where they stood in the ratings. *Lassie*, *Hogan's Heroes*, and the Andies – Griffith and Williams – all were gone at season's end. *The Beverly Hillbillies*, arguably the most popular TV series of the 1960s, got the pink slip after its ninth season. What happened?

CBS, which had ruled the roost so long and was anxious to continue to do so, took the lead in remaking prime time. It would be the last time that a single broadcast network would ever have that much power over American culture. James Aubrey, who had masterminded the network's rural comedy tilt, was long gone from CBS. The type of shows he had cultivated, including *The Jim Nabors Hour*, *Mayberry RFD*, *Petticoat Junction*, and *Hee Haw*, were all in the Top Thirty when cancelled in 1970. When the last survivor of the movement, the inadvertently postmodern *Green Acres*, got its pink slip at the end of the 1971–2 season, not a single rural comedy – the pillar upon which CBS had built its dominance during the 1960s – was left on the air. Pat Buttram, who played Mr. Haney in *Green Acres*, put it this way in his perennially hoarse drawl: "Well those boys up there in the suits at CBS just cancelled every show that had a tree in it, and that was the long and the short of it."[3]

Instead of trees, viewers got Relevance. The increasing presence of women in the workforce was among the first contemporary themes to be taken up in this massive revision of prime-time stereotypes. The change in sitcom women is well illustrated in a comparison of two structurally similar sitcoms that appeared in chronological sequence. *That Girl* (ABC, 1966–71), though full of color and fashion, was rooted in the old television "career girl" sitcom, which dates back to such shows as *Private Secretary* and *Our Miss Brooks* in the 1950s. Ann Marie (Marlo Thomas), like an increasing number of American women, moves from a suburban family home to an apartment of her own in the big city so she can pursue a career. However, from the very first episode of the series, she is positioned under the watchful care of two men – her father and her fiancé. Together, they provide a safety net and a circumscription to the personal dangers and possibilities of her attempt to become a Broadway actress. Given the generic baggage the audience carries to the show, there is an implication hanging over it that one day Dad will give her away to her intended, Donald, and the delivery of 2.5 kids – not a Tony award – will be the comic, if not necessarily happy, ending.

The Mary Tyler Moore Show (CBS, 1970–7) revises the sitcom career girl by removing the male safety nets and circumscriptions. The men in the series provide no marriage possibilities. Mr. Grant is too old to be a romantic match for Mary and too full of his own problems to be anything more than something short of a father figure. Her co-worker Murray is married with children and, though much taken with Mary, he is thoroughly committed to living *la vida* pointedly *non loca*. Ted is vain, stupid, deceptive, and wealthy, and one out of four is not enough for the likes of an "It" girl like Mary, especially at that somewhat less philistine moment in American history.

Though we learn in one of the most turgid episodes in sitcom history that all three of Mary's male office friends harbor intense psycho-social fantasies about her, these remain otherwise suppressed. Mary, who is promoted from Mr. Grant's gopher to associate producer of WJM-TV's evening news program, goes out with a dozen or more guys over the course of the series. These trysts are given short shrift, however, and only a few last longer than an episode. Her job, her female *goombahs* (Rhoda and Georgette) and her female associates (Phyllis and Sue Ann), and an occasional date with a guest star stud muffin provide all the satisfaction she seems to require.

The racial picture of prime time was changing as well, with African American performers winning starring roles in prime-time shows for the first time since the early 1950s. The racial history of pre-cable TV, catalogued in detail by scholar and entrepreneur of the intellect J. Fred Macdonald in his book *Blacks and White TV*, is not a proud one. Following the 1952 cancellations of *Amos 'n' Andy* and *Beulah*, sitcoms whose humor depended on the racial stereotyping of African Americans were virtually absent from television, save a few servant roles, such as the hilarious domineering housekeeper played by Amanda Randolph in *Make Room For Daddy*. The only real exception during a thirteen-year prime-time lock-out of black talent was *The Nat King Cole Show* (NBC, 1956–7), but corporate advertisers were advised by their agencies that participation could result in product boycotts, especially in the Southern states where segregation remained legal, and this doomed the show to an undeserved cancellation.

This situation began to change with the success of Bill Cosby as the co-star (with white actor Robert Culp), of *I Spy* (NBC, 1965–8), which rode in on the espionage wave that had started in the cinema with the James Bond series and spilled over into television during the mid-1960s. *Julia* (NBC, 1968–71), as mentioned above, broke the color barrier in situation comedy in 1968, and *The Flip Wilson Show* did likewise in comedy-variety in 1970.

Flip Wilson, finishing second in the overall Nielsens to *All in the Family* in its first full season, can also be seen as part of a mini-revival of TV comedy-variety which, like its theatrical predecessor vaudeville, died an extremely long death, with no one ever quite willing to pull the plug on the respirator. Wilson, though not overtly political in his material, broke through many long-standing boundaries in content with his repertoire of characters. The most shocking of these to the audiences of the period was Geraldine, a sassy, outspoken woman who reveled in testing the limits of female propriety, a sharp contrast to the slapstick misogyny that Milton Berle had brought to TV transvestism in the early 1950s.

Other Wilson creations included the high-spirited and presciently shifty Reverend LeRoy, minister of the Church of What's Happening Now; and Freddie the Playboy, a silver-tongued ladies' man, updated some twenty years later by Tim Meadows on *Saturday Night Live*. With Wilson's injections of racial (though not racist) humor and sexual (though not erotic) humor, the genre showed more life than it had in a decade or more under the watch of aging banana-peel meisters such as Red Skelton and Jackie Gleason, or slo-mo crooners such as Perry Como and Andy Williams.

The short-lived revival of vaudeo also included *The Smothers Brothers Comedy Hour* (CBS, 1967–9), which was abruptly cancelled before its time for going too far in its anti-Vietnam War material, especially when Tom and Dick presented black-listed Communist folksinger Pete Seeger. What were they thinking? The show's breakthrough pot jokes, anti-clerical humor, and political double-talk routines smoothed the way for the vaudeo revival's biggest hit, *Rowan and Martin's Laugh-In* (NBC, 1968–73).

Laugh-In began as a summer replacement for *The Dean Martin Show*, which was mostly powered by drunk jokes, leggy chorus girls, and guest shots by surviving Rat Pack[4] singers and stand-ups. Hosted by Dan Rowan and Dick Martin, a comedy team not well known outside of California, the show did score some ratings points in its temporary spot and was moved to its own prime-time slot in the fall of 1968. It surprised everyone by becoming the first non-sitcom comedy series to hit number 1 in the ratings since Berle had done it twenty years before.[5] *Laugh-In* was full of jokes about specific events, issues and styles of the day, all of which make it virtually incomprehensible today to all but historians and the oldest professional TV critics. But the pace of its cutting, faster than anything yet seen in prime time, is quite recognizable by contemporary standards. Poet Allen Ginsberg, who claimed that he did not own a television at the time, enjoyed the show so much that he viewed it regularly at a neighborhood bar, characterizing *Laugh-In* as "psychedelic slapstick of an unusually high order."[6]

The success of *Laugh-In* in the ratings – three number 1 seasons in a row – put the NBC Program Standards office on the defensive in censorship squabbles. But the show could actually be very subtle in its technique, especially on political issues. Having ridiculed Richard Nixon dozens of times during the 1968 presidential campaign, producer George Schlatter invited him to come on the show. Ostensibly a gesture of friendly fairness, Nixon's appearance actually gave him the opportunity to successfully ridicule himself. It took no less a student of the role of television in American politics than Bill Clinton to revive the technique, with his appearances on television entertainment programs in 1992.

Laugh-In can also be used as a barometer for the changing boundaries of sexual display on prime-time television. In 1965, for example, NBC had balked at showing Barbara Eden's bare midriff in *I Dream of Jeannie*. Just three years later, Goldie Hawn was doing the Watusi weekly on *Laugh-In,* with a peace sign painted around her bellybutton. Though tattoos were still considered the province of sailors, or even salty sailors, during this period, art was then, as now, nothing if not transformation.

Where comedy goes on prime-time TV, genre drama is likely to follow. Aaron Spelling, then enjoying his little-remembered crimeshow period, introduced

African American cop heroes in such hits such as *The Mod Squad* (ABC, 1968–73) and *The Rookies* (ABC, 1972–6). Female officers included the *Squad's* Julie Barnes (Peggy Lipton), as well as the doughty Eve Whitfield (Barbara Anderson) of *Ironside* (NBC, 1967–75) and the spicy Pepper Anderson (Angie Dickinson) of *Police Woman* (NBC, 1974–8). The hearts of young white liberal attorneys could be seen visibly bleeding on *The Bold Ones* (NBC, 1969–73), and *The Young Lawyers* (ABC, 1970–1).

Curiously, the only show from the Relevance period that managed to survive the end of the twentieth century in production is probably the one that seemed least likely to succeed at the time of its debut: *60 Minutes* (CBS, 1968–). Although it would eventually spend dozens of seasons as a popular show (including four as Nielsen's number 1), its early ratings dragged the proud mantle of CBS News straight to the bottom of the heap. It took seven years and more audience studies than a sitcom project pitched by favorite relatives of a network president to reckon that if *60 Minutes* was placed after NFL football on Sunday nights, dutiful American parents would force both themselves and their kids to watch it.

TV's pre-Oprah makeover from Rural to Relevant during the 1970s accomplished its primary goal: attracting young adults. A new generation of advertising executives, unimpressed with the sheer bulk of the audiences that national broadcasting had been delivering regularly on radio and television for half a century, were beginning to demand demographic profiles of the massive pile of heads they were paying for. No characteristic interested them more than age. Advertisers wanted young adults, not only because they tended to know less about rationally managing their finances, but because their relentless, hormone-driven pursuit of packaged identities tended to make them more susceptible to suggestions about how to deal with what their elders had concluded were the intractable problems of life on this fallen planet.

As if the organic impulsiveness of youth had not proved itself a loose enough cannon over the course of the millennia, it was now being supercharged, for the first time, with the mass-offer credit card. Maturity? Prudence? Judgment? Who needed the headaches? Let the bearers of such burdens watch *60 Minutes*, *Murder, She Wrote*, and *Prescription: Murder*. Some cultures practice ancestor worship; America chose descendant worship, providing a box full of household gods to the faithful.

As Real As It Got

When it comes to American television history, the sitcom is the genre of record, and indeed no program captured the spirit of the Relevance period more than *All in the Family* (CBS, 1971–9). Norman Lear, the show's creator-producer, unlocked the Victorian birdcage that situation comedy had been perched in since its birth during the radio era, freeing it into what had been the forbidden forests of modernist

Homosexuality comes to prime time: *That Certain Summer* (ABC, 1972)

Any discussion of the Relevance era would be incomplete without mention of how it was manifest in the made-for-television movie, which introduced dozens of "hot" topics to prime times in areas such as race, gender, and sexuality. *That Certain Summer*, produced by Richard Levinson and William Link, concerned the relationship between a divorced gay father and his straight son. They spend a vacation together each summer, but the father has, until now, remained closeted. It was the first entertainment program to appear on American commercial television that included frankly homosexual characters. In a 1996 interview, Link recalls the circumstances surrounding the production of the film:

WILLIAM LINK. My late partner, Dick Levinson, and I got that idea while we were at Universal. . . . One day we went over to pick up a gay friend of ours, a director named Don, for lunch. There's this freckled kid in the office, a face right out of middle America. I said to the secretary, "Who's that kid?" and she answers, "Oh, that's Don's son." I said, "Yeah, but Don's gay, isn't he?" And [she says,] "Oh yeah, the kid is from his previous marriage." And Dick and I said to each other "Boy, this would make a terrific drama. But how will we ever do it on television? No one's gonna touch this. Maybe we'll do it Off-Broadway or for Broadway." So we broached it to an assistant of Barry Diller. Barry Diller was running the *ABC Movie-of-the-Week*. Barry said, "I really like this idea and I think you should do it on ABC." We said, "Oh, my God," and we wrote a script and he liked it. I don't know the real-life demons he had to fight at the network. We weren't privy to that information. All we knew was Barry would move heaven and earth to make this picture about a gay father. That's all we needed to know. We were dealing with the top guy. He was head of "movies-of-the-week" at ABC. But we also had to [deal with] these two shrinks who ABC consulted on content of their movies. They were both from Philly. They were impossible. And we meet with these guys and they say, "Well, you're gonna have to, at one point, say 'If I could be anything else rather than a homosexual . . . I would be.'" We got into awful trouble.

DAVID MARC. Were these consulting psychologists picked by ABC precisely because they would say that?

Sidebar 7.3 (cont.)

WL. I don't know. These guys were terrible. We had meetings with these guys and Barry. These guys were so repressive. At meetings they were saying, "Oh, you know how they make love. They go up each other's asses." And Barry was sitting there, sweating. You could see it. . . . He had a silk shirt on. It was terrible. We felt sorry for Barry. The shrinks also said, "You've got to put in one character who speaks for heterosexual America." So we put in the brother-in-law, the Martin Sheen character, Gary McClain, and . . . he made a speech at the end [saying that] if he had his pick, he wouldn't be gay. We got into a lot of trouble with gay publications with that, even though they generally got behind the movie and they liked the movie.

DM. At that point, the very mention of the subject must have been considered a real "step."

WL. We got a lot of letters after the show. One was from a gay young man who said, "I was gonna commit suicide. I was in despair. And I turned on the set and I said, 'Oh my God. This TV show is sympathetic to gay characters!'" He said it changed his life.

DM. So there's the power of television.

WL. We won no awards or Emmys for producing or for the screenplay of *That Certain Summer*, but we were very proud of it. I have got to tell you, it was the best of the year; it should have won. Everybody said it. But the [television] Academy simply would not give it to us. We got other kinds of awards though. Years later, a gay man, a guy who has been in the industry a long time, said, "*That Certain Summer* was the beginning of tolerance in the media. I don't know how these guys got this picture on, but they got it on."

DM. Given those circumstances, would you say that Hal Holbrook was brave to take the leading role of the gay character?

WL. Yes. We were turned down by Cliff Robertson, who said "I'd rather play Hitler." And he wasn't the only one who wouldn't go near it. We had bomb threats to ABC affiliates before the show went on.

William Link, interviewed by David Marc at his home in Beverly Hills, California, November 15, 1996. Audiotape and transcription, Steven H. Scheuer Collection in Television History, Center for the Study of Popular Television, Syracuse University Library. Copyright Syracuse University 1999.

content. War, sexual violence, racism, labor problems, even death itself, became the stuff of commercially interrupted 30-minute episodic comic television drama.

Shot on videotape rather than film, *All in the Family* went so far as to visually suggest the gripping realism of a daytime soap opera viewed in mixed company. Perhaps most jarring of all to its weekly audience of about 35 million was the show's televisually unfamiliar language. Though the swear words and racial epithets are mild to the point of being hardly noticeable by post-cable standards, the context was such for 1972 viewers that an *All in the Family* "damn" thundered across a 19-inch SONY Trinitron like a latter-day HBO "motherfucker." The word "colored" could provoke the shocked reaction of "nigger" being said today by a middle-class white in a college classroom. For the first time in sitcom history, an onscreen warning was deemed necessary to protect the faint of heart from the fury of the sitcom.

Archie Bunker (Carroll O'Connor) is a loud, ill-mannered bigot who resents the changing attitudes of his nation and the changing demographics of his neighborhood. As he sees it, he has led a reasonably good life since the end of the Second World War, working by day as a loading-dock foreman, and sitting home at night on his paternal throne in front of the TV set. He is attended to by his daffy but docile wife Edith (Jean Stapleton) and he is obeyed by his college-age daughter Gloria (Sally Struthers). Comedy emerged from invasions of Archie's American dream life by forces both within and without.

Gloria marries Mike Stivic (Rob Reiner), a sociology graduate student full of post-Darwin ideas, who moves in until he finishes his degree. (Then, as now, those dissertations could take forever.) Throughout the series, the cultural jousting between Ancient Archie and Modern Mike becomes the vehicle for vulgarized dialogues on every social, political, and aesthetic debate raging in the America imagined by sitcom writers. As if a fifth column in his very own castle is not threatening enough to Archie, a second front is opened when an African American family, the Jeffersons, buy the house next door.

All in the Family was the highest-rated show on television for five consecutive years beginning with the season of 1971–2. Furthermore it begat a clutch of ideologically related spin-offs that hovered in the Top Ten with it: *Maude*, a paean to the discreet charms of an oft-divorced menopausal limousine liberal; *The Jeffersons*, which catapulted Archie's neighbors of color from striver respectability to the satisfying embarrassments of an Upper East Side "deluxe apartment in the sky"; *One Day at a Time*, the pop culture debut of the heroic "divorced – with kids" soccer mom; and *Good Times*, a tale of life in the Chicago projects that was, ironically, the didactic runt of the litter.

The Lear hits were complemented on the CBS schedule by a series of sophisticoms produced by MTM Enterprises, another independent production studio. These included *The Mary Tyler Moore Show*, *The Bob Newhart Show*, *Rhoda*, *Phyllis*, and others, all of which focused on the depiction of the manners and mores of post-1960s middle-class America. Until recently the home of *Gomer Pyle*, CBS now became the purveyor of *M*A*S*H*, a Vietnam era anti-war sitcom diplomatically set as a parable in the ancient history of the Korean War.[7]

Though Lear dominated the Relevance moment in terms of spirit and ratings, the overtly political subject matter of his programs proved to be a passing fancy of mass taste that would not outlast the 1970s. MTM developed a variety of forms and styles for dealing with contemporary subject matter and human relations that wielded a much greater collective influence over the future development of television programming. Though the studio had been formed to produce sitcoms, it moved into other genres, adapting the speed of situation dialogue and comedy cutting to other kinds of prime-time storytelling. The results were vital rehabilitations of tired old TV formulas.

The first successful MTM hour-long dramas was a pair of reasonably realistic social urban fantasies: *Lou Grant* (CBS, 1978–82), concerning a muckraking Los Angeles newspaper, and *The White Shadow* (CBS, 1978–81), an inner-city high school set-up built upon the racial bridge of the American basketball court. Both stood out as adult and socially conscious, seeming like spiritual remnants of old-time 1950s anthology teletheater, especially when compared to the more popular hour-longs of the period, such as *The Dukes of Hazzard* and *Fantasy Island*.

But MTM's real breakthroughs were yet to follow. *Hill Street Blues* (NBC, 1981–7), a police show, and *St. Elsewhere* (NBC, 1982–8), a medical series, infused the energy of the studio's sitcom writing *and* the civic-mindedness of *Lou Grant* and *White Shadow* into the emotional morass of the multi-plotted, continuing-story, night-time soap opera, à la *Dallas* and *Dynasty*. The result was more than a style, but a kind of *modus operandi* for intelligent, engaging TV whose influence remains apparent decades later, especially in such HBO series as *Oz*, *The Sopranos*, *The Wire*, and *Sex and the City*.

There have been books written about the "MTM style."[8] What's worth noting here is that, when MTM entered television in the 1970s, the medium was obsessed with content battles between producers (e.g., Lear, Schlatter, Gelbart) who wanted to do fresh, new, realistic work, and network executives, who had been weaned on the wisdom of least objectionable programming. The producers won many of these battles, and the rest were resolved in the late 1980s by the need to compete with cable.

MTM was the first television production house to look beyond these episode-by-episode battles over specific words and topics and show an understanding of the general direction in which television might go as a dramatic art in the 1980s. Under Grant Tinker and his successors, writers and producers were afforded opportunities to take advantage of the newly won freedoms to conceptualize new ways of intelligent storytelling that were specifically designed for television. Some thirty years after the fact, Norman Lear programs look like videotaped theater pieces and *Laugh-In* looks like yet another of the many attempts to revive beloved vaudeville. A rerun of MTM's *St. Elsewhere*, however, looks not much different from *ER*,

Chicago Hope, or other latter-day medical television. It is perhaps more accurate to say that the more recent shows look like *St. Elsewhere*.

Writers and producers who were either trained at MTM or liberated by the new styles explored by its hits would go on to create or produce dozens of the most satisfying shows of their eras. Examples of sitcoms influenced by MTM aesthetics and production ancestry include *Taxi*, *Cheers*, *Brothers*, *Frasier*, and *The Simpsons*; dramas include the hour-longs of such executive producers as Steven Bochco (*LA Law*, *NYPD Blue*, et al.), Dick Wolf (*Law and Order*) and Tom Fontana (*Homicide*).[9]

Regulation and Social Effects

The television industry gave extensive coverage to the Vietnam War in the late 1960s and early 1970s. Proponents of the war, both then and now, blame television for turning public opinion against it, while opponents of the war tend to refuse to give television any such high credit. In any case, Vietnam was the first extensively televised war. As American troop concentrations grew and body counts spiraled, audiences took a greater interest in it, boosting the ratings for news and creating controversies over coverage, even though not a single bomb had a camera mounted on its nose.

In a 1969 speech (which was broadcast on television), Vice-President Spiro *"nolo contendere"* Agnew, the oft-forgotten first of the Nixon–Agnew ticket to run askance of the law, attacked network news for what he saw as a biased interpretations of events. Calling news commentators "nattering nabobs of negativism," the alliterative Agnew complained that just a handful of journalists and producers, working for just three companies, were determining what the entire population of the country was learning about national and international events. (He had a point there.) He was especially critical of the practice the networks made of providing "instant analyses" directly after presidential speeches. Though Agnew lacked formal training, when it comes to television, everyone's a critic.

The most controversial battle in the Nixon administration's war with the press over press coverage of the war was over a documentary, *The Selling of the Pentagon* (CBS, 1971). Though it had been dormant for most of the 1960s, the old CBS muckraking spirit came out of the closet for a last hurrah. The documentary shot holes in US government propaganda concerning the war, and exposed a relationship between the Pentagon and its corporate contractors that smacked of war profiteering – this during a period when body-bags containing American soldiers were a daily part of the evening news.

Controversy over the show led to a congressional investigation into the production of television documentaries, and that, of course, meant an investigation into the three network news departments that turned them out. Congressman Harley Staggers (D – West Virginia), chairman of the House Judiciary Committee, went so far as to demand that CBS submit production materials to his committee, including outtakes not used in the actual program. When CBS president Frank Stanton refused, Staggers threatened to put him in jail. Though Stanton – and the rights of TV journalists – was upheld in court, the incident illustrates the power that the broadcasting industry could wield in the 1970s, licenses or not.

Stanton found support for his position among journalists in all media as well as among a variety of civic and religious organizations. But *The Selling of the Pentagon* victory did not usher in a new age of muckraking documentaries. The result, if

SIDEBAR 7.4

The selling of the Pentagon

Frank Stanton, then president of the CBS television network, recalls his decision, at the threat of jail, to refuse to yield CBS News outtakes and reporters' notes to the House Judiciary Committee, which was investigating the documentary *The Selling of the Pentagon*.

"It was no big deal. It's what my mother taught me. It was not a difficult decision. I felt very deeply that, under the First Amendment, Congress should keep its cotton-picking fingers off us. No question about it. I promised my colleagues that I was going to do everything I could to win this thing because it was important for broadcast news that we come as close to First Amendment protection as we can have it. In fact, I said one day on the stand in Congress to the Staggers Committee, 'If I were a newspaper publisher, we wouldn't be here.' The answer was, 'You're not. You don't have that freedom; you're *licensed*. Therefore, we're going to put the finger on you.' Well, they didn't use those exact words, but that was the attitude. So I knew it was going to be tough. I knew that I had to get all of our affiliates to support the position we were taking and use their cooperation in getting the votes lined up in Congress. It was a tough period, lasting roughly from February to, I guess, July. Did I have any question how it was going to come out? Yes, I was very concerned. A Congressman called me on a Sunday morning and said, 'Can't you think of something that you can give Staggers so he'll pull back?' I said, 'I can't think of any way you can have the First Amendment and start chipping away at it. Either you have it or you don't have it.'"

Frank Stanton, interviewed by David Marc, New York City, May 21, 1999. Audiotape and transcription, Steven H. Scheuer Collection in Television History, Center for the Study of Popular Television, Syracuse University Library. Copyright Syracuse University, 1999.

KEN BURNS

Ken Burns has produced a large body of documentary films that has reached the public primarily through public television. They include *The Brooklyn Bridge* (1981), *Huey Long* (1985), and *Frank Lloyd Wright* (1998). His week-long mini-series, such as *The Civil War* (1989), *Baseball* (1994), and *Jazz* (2000), have stimulated national discussions on aspects of American history, a rare achievement for documentaries. Here Burns disputes the oft-made assertion (and assumption) that he is a historian.

"I'm a filmmaker. That's what I do for a living. I'm not a historian or I'm an amateur historian at best. I am practicing in history as a painter might choose oils or watercolors. As a filmmaker, I'm interested in the art of film. So I shoot on film; I edit on film; I finish on film. But, at the last moment, it is transferred to this videotape medium and distributed. I gravitated there for two reasons. One was fairly practical. It seemed to be where the money was to support the kind of historical investigations that seemed to be piquing my interest at the beginning of my professional life. But also it was the largest classroom I knew. I don't mean that in a proselytizing way. It was just possible to reach a lot of people and to initiate a conversation that could really have an influence. It's not enough to just make a splash at a film festival where a few hundred people see it and get tucked away in a niche of whatever degree of respect. It was important to move. I've said many times that I feel I'm an emotional archeologist; that the evidence of the past, however dry and dusty it might be, comes alive when there is an emotional connection from then to now. That's what I've looked for in all the work."

Ken Burns was interviewed by David Marc, Walpole, New Hampshire, October 2, 1998. Video DVD and transcription, Steven H. Scheuer Collection in Television History, Center for the Study of Popular Television, Syracuse University Library. Copyright Syracuse University 1999.

anything, was to make the networks even more timid in their choice of subject matter. There was simply too much money to be made in prime time. Situations such as the one created by *The Selling of the Pentagon* were to be avoided; interviews with movie stars on *60 Minutes* were much to be preferred. "I don't recall anybody in the business community coming to my support," Stanton said. "They were not going the other way either; they were just indifferent."

Several major regulatory actions were taken by the federal government during the 1970s, none of which the business community was crazy about:

- After a protracted period of debate, cigarette advertising on television was banned by federal legislation as of January 2, 1971 (this allowed one last day of cigarette selling during the bowl games). The controversy over tobacco advertising had begun with the Surgeon General's *Report on the Effects of Smoking and Tobacco* in 1964, which was the first official US government suggestion of the health risks involved. Like most advertisers faced with censorship, the tobacco companies tended to react with a "free speech" defense.

  The situation intensified in 1967 when the FCC ruled that, based on its Fairness Doctrine, anti-smoking messages should be allowed free air time on television stations to balance advertisements by tobacco companies. When a complete ban on cigarette advertising was suggested by the Federal Trade Commission a year later, broadcasters protested wildly. Ten percent of total TV advertising revenues came from cigarette and other tobacco advertising at that time. The tobacco companies themselves were more willing to go along with the idea, believing that a voluntary withdrawal from television and radio advertising would keep the FTC from banning them from all mass media venues. Moreover, they recognized that, since all cigarette companies would be subject to the restrictions, they might actually save money without losing market share to their competitors.

- The prime-time access rule came into effect in September 1971 to encourage the production of local and independent television programming. By the mid-1960s, the prime viewing hours were almost completely locked up by newly expanded editions of both local and network news, and by a network prime-time schedule that ran from 7.30 p.m. to 11 p.m. EST. The prime-time access rule allowed networks to provide programming for only three hours per evening in prime time (four hours on Sundays), with the intent that this would open 30 minutes per evening to local and independent programming. All three networks relinquished the 7.30–8.00 p.m. slot, the prime-time segment with the smallest audiences. Most local stations, however, elected to air nationally syndicated programming during this time period rather than less profitable local productions.

- The financial interest and syndication rules (fin-syn) were created at the same time as the prime-time access rule. These rules forbade networks from retaining any financial interests, including those derived from syndication rights, in any programs that they did not own entirely. Since the networks held some financial interest in 98 percent of the programming they aired in 1970, the concessions demanded by the fin-syn rules were substantial. By 1975, further restrictions were handed down, limiting the number of hours a network could fill with programs they themselves produced and owned. Starting at two and a half hours of entertainment programming per week in prime time (later moving up to five) and eight hours in the daytime, the rule was designed to expire in 1990, and it was repealed in 1995.

- Although the FCC is forbidden to regulate the content of television, an important attempt at "self-regulation" surfaced in the mid-1970s. In 1975 Richard Wiley, the chairman of the FCC, allegedly encouraged the networks to limit violent programming to time slots after 9 p.m. EST. Arthur Taylor, the president of CBS, became the chief advocate of what became known as "family viewing time" (8–9 p.m., as far as the networks were concerned), and he enlisted the support of the other networks as well. Producers, on the other hand, were not so eager to offer their support. Among other things, they were concerned that the family viewing time agreement would restrict the times in which stations could air their shows in syndication. *All in the Family*'s producer Norman Lear, who at the time had several shows airing on the networks between 8 and 9 p.m. that might have been deemed inappropriate for family viewing time, led the attack on the idea, claiming that the First Amendment had been compromised by Wiley's advocating such an agreement and that the networks had stepped into anti-trust violations by conspiring to make it happen. A Los Angeles federal district court disallowed the "family viewing time" self-regulatory action in 1976.

- The issue of television violence re-emerged in the early 1970s with the publication in 1972 of the five-volume report of the Surgeon General's Scientific Advisory Committee on Television and Social Behavior. The Surgeon General told a Senate committee that "the overwhelming consensus and the unanimous Scientific Advisory Committee's report indicates that televised violence, indeed, does have an adverse effect on certain members of our society." The report encouraged remedial action, but the FCC, limited by the First Amendment, took no action until 1996, at which time it mandated a ratings system to inform parents of programs that might be inappropriate for children.

Over the next decade, however, several important cases were tried in the courts that addressed the relationship between violence on TV and violent behavior among television viewers. In *Zamora et al.* v. *Columbia Broadcasting System et al.* (1979), the parents of a 15-year-old boy who killed his 83-year-old neighbor sued a television network for "intoxicating" their son with TV violence. In 1981, the complainants in *Niemi* v. *National Broadcasting Company* argued that the mechanics of a brutal rape were learned on a made-for-TV movie called *Born Innocent* (NBC, 1974). Other cases, not directly related to violent behavior, sought to hold television broadcasters responsible for behavior learned on their programs. A boy who was partially blinded while performing an experiment demonstrated on *The Mickey Mouse Club* was the subject of *Walt*

Disney Productions et al. v. *Shannon et al.* (1981). In *DeFilippo* v. *National Broadcasting Company et al.* (1982), a parent sued NBC after a son hanged himself while imitating a stunt man's demonstration he'd seen on *The Tonight Show*.

Programming and the Television Industry

The significant critical and commercial success of Relevance programming in the 1970s opened television to entirely new areas of content. Though timely topics have remained a principal source of story ideas, it is worth noting that, by the middle of the 1970s, a kind of backlash against them was becoming evident. A changing cultural climate, ushered in by the defeat in Vietnam and the Watergate scandals, led some network executives and television producers to believe that audiences might be ready for a return to escapist programming.

In the 1976–7 season, *All in the Family* gave up its five-year reign at the top of the ratings to *Happy Days* (ABC, 1974–84), a high school comedy starring Ron Howard, a former cast member of *The Andy Griffith Show*. *Happy Days* was set in the 1950s, establishing the decade as the nostalgic time before the Watergate complex was built and before most Americans had heard of Vietnam. Other such hits included the *Happy Days* spin-off, *Laverne & Shirley* (ABC, 1976–83), which was set in the early 1960s, and *Little House on the Prairie* (NBC, 1974–83), set in the late nineteenth century. As its title suggests, *Happy Days* suggested an older philosophy of television: family hi-jinx and broadly played slapstick, with storylines divorced from disturbing features of the so-called real world.

The escapist fare of the late 1970s, however, was not the same as that which had dominated in the days before *All in the Family*. The Jeannie had been put back in the bottle. The Relevance programs had brought on a relaxation of industry and public attitudes toward the kind of content that was deemed appropriate for broadcast TV. The new escapism took advantage of that openness not so much to portray controversial social issues as to present a more sexually oriented revisiting of the old TV material. Before 1970, even married couples on screen had been shown sleeping in separate beds.

Whereas CBS had led the networks in the development of Relevance programming in the early 1970s, ABC would take the lead in the last half of the decade under its renowned President of Entertainment, Fred Silverman (who had come over from CBS). The trend toward greater sexuality soon found names in the popular press: "jiggle TV" in the more polite publications; "T&A TV" elsewhere. These programs tended to feature young, attractive women and, increasingly, men as well, in stories that often required them to dress in a scanty or provocative manner. Perhaps most accurately, characters were dressed scantily in the hope that they would be provocative.

The Love Boat (ABC, 1977–86) was a romantic comedy that took place on a cruise ship; *Charlie's Angels* (ABC, 1976–81) presented three female detectives who specialized in undercover investigations that required them to disguise themselves in beachwear, nightwear, and similarly revealing attire; *Three's Company* (ABC, 1977–84) followed the then titillating premise of two young women and a man sharing an apartment; *Fantasy Island* (ABC, 1978–84) was set on a tropical island where people came to have their dreams fulfilled. These were more often romantic than erotic.

By the end of the decade, *Mary Tyler Moore* and *All in the Family* were gone and *M*A*S*H* had gone into its gothic post-psychoanalysis period. Based in large part on its nostalgia–jiggle programming combo, ABC had arrived as the top-rated network for the first time in its history. This once unimaginable achievement was largely the work of two producers: Garry Marshall, producer-creator of *Happy Days*, *Laverne and Shirley*, and other hit sitcoms, and Aaron Spelling, whose productions included *Charlie's Angels*, *The Love Boat*, and *Fantasy Island*.

But perhaps ABC's most memorable success of the 1970s was the work of a former documentary producer, David Wolper. *Roots* was a twelve-hour adaptation of Alex Haley's novel, aired across eight consecutive nights in January 1977. It was based on Haley's family history, beginning with the capture of his ancestors in West Africa in the eighteenth century, following them through slavery and finally to emancipation in America. That year, all eight installments made the list of the fifty highest-rated programs of all time, including the finale, which was, at that time, the highest-rated TV show in history. The critical and industry reception was just as strong. The National Academy of Television Arts and Sciences gave the mini-series an unprecedented thirty-seven Emmy award nominations.

Roots was the quintessential product of the Relevance period, a program that could never have been aired before it. Even in 1977 it was the object of controversy. Some viewers and organizations took issue with the show's scenes of partial nudity (a first on a network drama program), with its rape scene, and with its frank presentation of the horrors of slavery, including whippings and other forms of brutal violence. Others even complained of historical inaccuracies.

Roots helped establish the mini-series as a vibrant television form, though it wasn't the first American mini-series, or even the longest. ABC had aired a successful twelve-hour adaptation of *Rich Man, Poor Man*, an Irwin Shaw novel, the previous season. The phenomenal ratings success of *Roots*, however, guaranteed the immediate future of the historical mini-series. Over the next decade, a shelf-full of historical novels would be adapted for television in this way, including *Shogun* (NBC, 1980), *The Thorn Birds* (ABC, 1983), *The Winds of War* (ABC, 1983), and the twenty-six-hour-long *Centennial* (NBC, 1978). Like just about everything else on television, and in life, success does not last forever. Escalating production budgets and falling ratings eventually caught up with the mini-series and it too became history.

Notes

1 Ken Burns, producer, *Empire of the Air: The Men Who Made Radio* (Alexandria, VA: PBS Video; Radio Pioneers Film Project, Inc., ca. 1991).

2 Clifton Webb (1889–1966) was a quintessential upper-middle-class father-figure in mid-twentieth-century films such as *Cheaper by the Dozen* (1950) and *Mister Scoutmaster* (1953).

3 Remark attributed to Pat Buttram by Ruth Henning in David Marc, "Interview with Paul and Ruth Henning" [Sound Recording], September 9, 1996, Television Oral History Archive, Syracuse University Copyright Syracuse University, 1999. Language has been embellished with the habits of the speaker.

4 "Rat Pack" refers to a group of male entertainers, including such figures as Frank Sinatra, Dean Martin, Peter Lawford, Sammy Davis Jr., and Joey Bishop, who were mythologized for their drunken debauchery and sexual escapades. The film *Oceans 11* (1960), directed by Lewis Milestone, is recommended, as is the 2001 remake, directed by Steven Soderberg and starring George Clooney and Brad Pitt. Also see *Rat Pack* (HBO, 2002).

5 See David Marc, *Comic Visions: Television Comedy and American Culture*, 2nd edn (Boston: Blackwell, 1997), pp. 118–23, for a detailed account of the two programs.

6 Allen Ginsberg, lecture/reading, State University of New York at Binghamton, April 5, 1971.

7 The Korean War (1950–2) occurred before US troop involvement in the Vietnam War (1956–74).

8 Jane Feuer, Tise Vahimagi, and Paul Kerr (eds), *MTM: "Quality Television"* (London: British Film Institute Books, 1984).

9 For a detailed discussion of television drama during this period, see Robert J. Thompson, *Television's Second Golden Age* (New York: Continuum, 1996).

~ 8 ~
OLIGOPOLY LOST AND FOUND

"I thought, as many religious people did, that television was a force for evil; that it was bringing a culture of materialism into the homes of America. But then I began to realize that television is neutral. Film is neutral. Radio is neutral. It's a question of who is in control of it, of who does the programming. It can be used for incredible good, for education, for spiritual uplift, for communication of values and ideas; or it can be used to destroy people. So it just is a question of what motive is behind the person using the medium."[1]

Pat Robertson, founding CEO, Christian Broadcasting Network

"If Paul Lazarsfeld and I and others hadn't done a lot of work in audience research, the agencies and the advertisers would have done it. It's as inevitable as anything that they had to find out who was listening and why."[2]

Dr. Frank Stanton, first president of the CBS television network

In 1948 most Americans were still listening to radio during the prime hours of the evening, just as they had been for some twenty years. The networks were still broadcasting a "full service" radio schedule consisting of dramas, situation comedies, variety shows, news, documentaries, dance music, and other popular genres of mass entertainment. Nevertheless, as David Sarnoff, William Paley, and a few hundred other radio executives knew, the handwriting was already on the screen for many of the special aural arts that had been evolving in broadcasting since the 1920s – especially aural drama.

The FCC had, by 1948, issued 108 licenses for television stations, and by the fall of that election year the three major companies that operated national radio networks – NBC, CBS, and ABC – were each feeding several hours of television service, on a daily basis, to tiny strings of stations concentrated in corridors of large cities located in the Northeast, the midwestern Great Lakes belt, and California. Appliance stores and catalog houses were stocking sets. Roof antennas were adding peculiar grid-like shapes to the national skyline for their thirty-year moment in the sun. It was a time for 300-ohm wire and vertical hold controls.

Television had not yet "arrived" in any grand sense, nor would it ever have a "coming out" ceremony beyond the razzmatazz that had accompanied its brief unveiling at the 1939 New York World's Fair. It didn't need one. The medium was a differential improvement on what people were already used to. It was well along in a seamless integration into a system of nationally coordinated culture that had already become so familiar to the long-entertained peoples of twentieth-century North America that it seemed natural.

Magazines had been slipping organized commerce under the door of home since the nineteenth century, and radio had been penetrating the walls with geometrically more of the same since the 1920s. The Madison Avenue broadcasting and Hollywood film industries had collaborated in providing Americans with a national mythology whose appeal seemed to transcend the subcultural barriers of what was otherwise an increasingly diverse population. Television came not as a revolution, but as a culmination. It animated the still photography of *Life* magazine, gave flesh to Jack Benny's radio voice, and brought the sexy people of the movies home – right into the bedroom, if you wanted – all in one fell swoop. The transfer of cultural power from church, school, and family to the customer service department was becoming a fact on the ground in the early days of TV, awaiting the improvements of cable via satellite, the personal computer, and the collapse of effective secular opposition to unbridled capitalism.

That summer, for the first time, the nominating conventions of the Democratic and Republican parties were carried not only on radio, but on television as well. The cast: President Harry S. Truman, the haberdasher from Missouri who, at this writing, still holds the record, asterisk-free, for dropping atomic bombs on civilian populations, was the Democrat. Truman pledged in his re-election campaign to bring the New Deal to a next logical step: universal health care (known then, by both proponents and critics, as "socialized medicine"). His Republican opponent was Governor Thomas E. Dewey of New York, a crime-busting DA who, at this writing, remains the last serious candidate for the big job on Pennsylvania Avenue to sport facial hair. Dewey was favored by most pollsters to win the election and thus prevent a Democratic Party five-peat. He ran on a Republican Party platform that pledged to dismantle the social security system as a crucial first step in recapturing the American economy for the free market after decades of New Deal Keynesianism.[3]

The baby television networks, though otherwise desperately short on content, chose not to cover the nominating conventions of any of the other political parties, despite the fact that two minor party candidates, arguably representative of two significant segments of the electorate, were also in the race: former vice-president Henry Wallace of Iowa, running on the American Labor Party ticket; and Senator Strom Thurmond of South Carolina of the segregationist States Rights Party (known more familiarly as the Dixiecrats), a splinter party formed by Southern Democrats who had walked out of the Democratic Party's 1948 convention when it adopted a platform plank, for the first time in major party history, expressly opposing legal segregation.

Truman won the election, but the Republicans took control of both houses of Congress for the first time since 1932. Neither the Democrats nor the Republicans were able to deliver their campaign promises; some sixty years later, universal health care and the government-mandated retirement system remain issues at the center of the American political agenda. As for the minor parties, their defeat and dissolution also tell tales. The political power and membership of American labor unions have since dwindled to fractions of what they had been during the first half of the twentieth century, and labor strikes are about as common as critters someone forgot to put on the endangered species list. As for racial segregation, the century-long Jim Crow regime that had followed the official banning of slavery has completely and utterly lost the force of law. Class-oriented and race-oriented movements have continued to assert influence over voting patterns since 1948, but both were placed, quite literally, "outside the box" of mainstream politics.[4]

Most Americans, by all accounts, have spent a good deal of their time since 1948 watching television. Barely half the population votes, and one can only imagine how many of those voters exercise the franchise with the enthusiasm of agnostics sitting in church for the sake of maintaining a self-consciously constructed personal illusion of general order.[5] Titanic historical events and political organizations continue to move people, but in most cases, that movement occurs to the right or to the left of their couches as they watch things "happen" on TV. If journalism is, as the saying goes, "the first draft of history," then we can be sure it is read more widely than the book.

Unbearable pressures – including racism, environmental degradation, the perceived disintegration of a workable social order – have moved some people to high levels of personal commitment and to take actions appropriate to their social beliefs. For others, however, the delights of the video screen – whether informed by broadcast, cable, direct satellite transmission, call-up, or broadband – have sufficed to max out the capacity for supra-televisual empathies. The video screen, whether embellished by the comforts of 24/7 climate control and spine-dulling furniture or enhanced by stimulation of illicit, over-the-counter or prescription pharmaceuticals, is compelling enough to satisfy a wide swath of the population.

Political scientists and sociologists who speak of "voter apathy" and who bemoan a lack of citizenship or moral backbone in the population/audience may well have missed a salient point as concerns the survivors of the age of broadcasting. Merely bearing daily witness – even bite-size, CNN-headline-size, daily witness – to the unending catalog of horrors announced in The News and re-enacted in The Entertainment may be more participation than *homo erectus* was built to withstand. To rise from the couch and actually go somewhere to vote for anybody might threaten some viewers with an assumption of guilt so frightening as to distance them from the grand ideals of the framers of the US Constitution, if they have been so lucky as to have been schooled in those ideals.

But that was "the broadcasting era," an age when people had their programs forcibly interrupted by "urgent messages" and even by planned presidential press conferences. Cable TV and the internet offer more news than ever, but they have removed the coercive burden of newswatching, thus enabling millions of viewers to abandon all contact with the collective mythologies of history, including the daily communion with history that we have come to call "the News." If people would rather be charmed by art than horrified by the world, who can blame them? Perhaps it is the news junkies who are dysfunctional.

The internet has, in fact, not disrupted the sheer craving for television viewing; in fact, surfing with a well-designed browser on a broadband connection is quite arguably the most addictive form of TV watching yet to reach the market. Asked in 2002 if the internet was having a negative impact on television viewing, Betsy Frank, head of research for the Viacom Corporation's MTV networks division replied, "What MTV viewers do less of, now that they are spending more time on the internet, is sleeping, talking and personal hygiene."[6] A Gallup poll conducted that same year found television to be "the single most popular way to spend an evening" among Americans, three times more popular than "seeing friends."[7] Why see friends when you can see *Friends* (NBC, 1994–2004)?

Is the internet a revolutionary force that has crossed the threshold of the *ancien régime* of broadcasting? Will the political stasis of American mass culture be broken by emerging forms of communication that will organize like-minded individuals into effective social and political units, such as seem to be emerging in the street demonstrations that accompany meetings of the World Bank board, the International Monetary Fund trustees, and other ruling juntas of the New World Order?

Or will social reality continue to fade into an increasingly distant mirage at the far end of what used to be known as social space? Is the unexplored expanse of cyberspace a pain-relieving diversion from the ecological and/or theological catastrophe that the remaining partisans of ideology have warned us we are hurtling toward – and that others have threatened to bring about no matter what we do?

We ask these questions not to answer them; rather, by declining to answer them, we honestly define the limits of our study. Instead, we choose to focus on what happened to television as it emerged from the womb of the broadcasting oligopoly that nurtured it from the laboratory to the living room.

The Train and the Station

We began this book by describing the practical separation of the act of communication from the realm of transportation, a pivotal sequence of events in human history that was launched by the invention of wired telegraphy in the nineteenth century (see chapter 1). We approach a conclusion by exploring a practical analogy between transportation and communication in contemporary America that may be of use in understanding how these two basic human activities remain bound to each other by that complex of problem-solving particulars that intellectuals are not too ashamed to call *culture*.

The relationship of radio and television broadcasting to American mass communication, circa Century-21, bears comparison to the relationship between railroad travel and American mass transportation since the 1950s. With the construction of the Interstate Highway System and the organization of air travel into a transcontinental hub-and-spoke mass transit system, the intercity passenger train gradually found itself pushed to the margins of an industry it had once dominated. No longer the imperious engine or symbol of American economy and culture, the passenger train was relegated to serving niche markets, such as megalopolitan center-city commuting and quality-time vacationing for those who continued to see value in viewing the nation's landscape, and doing so in the relative comfort of a vehicle that does not demand physical constraint or legally enforced sobriety as the price for speed. By the late 1960s it became apparent that highly visible government subsidies would play a necessary role if trains were to survive at all in the national transportation mix.[8]

This marginality was not the technologically determined "fate" of all intercity railroad passenger travel in the same way that the horse-drawn stagecoach had been made utterly obsolete by the passenger train. It was, rather, the result of consciously made political decisions in the United States that had the effect of withholding the necessary capital investment to keep American rail technology competitive with other forms of transport. Any doubt of this is dismissed with breathtaking speed by a 200-mile-per-hour train ride between Paris and Lyons or between Tokyo and Osaka.

An important factor in the disinvestment of the passenger train was that most American railroads were as anxious to leave the passenger business as the highway and aviation lobbies were to see them get out of it. The railroads preferred to concentrate their efforts on carrying uncomplaining potatoes and lumps of coal (see chapter 1).

The American broadcasting station today finds itself at the same kind of crossroads between viability and marginality that confronted the passenger train in the 1950s. Like the railroad station, the radio station debuted as a spectacular, transformative application of advanced technology and it was developed by private capital with the help of an extraordinary degree of government nurturing and protection. Each took less than a century to mature from a futurist "blue-sky" symbol into a workhorse industry at the heart of the national economy. In the case of the passenger train, it was technologically elbowed out by the automobile and the airplane into a kind of inglorious semi-retirement, where it sits today, forced to beg for a meager government pension so it can maintain a minimal surviving service, without which it faces oblivion. Are old-fashioned broadcasting stations – the kind that have studios and transmitting towers and a local news operation in Your Town or in a town nearby or at least in a town of some kind – heading for the same fate?

Just as the American transportation industry committed itself to the belief that people can now be delivered more profitably by means other than rail, the American communication industry seems to be coming to the conclusion that advertising (and what it takes to get people to attend to advertising) is more profitably delivered by single-source satellite transmissions than by hundreds of locally transmitted airborne signals.

In railroading, American corporations successfully divorced themselves from the human travel business in a compact hammered out by the Nixon administration in 1971 known as the National Railroad Passenger Act, the enabling legislation that created Amtrak. Since that time, Amtrak and a score of tax-funded regional commuter authorities have run virtually all scheduled passenger trains in the US. Broadcasting is by no means that far along in a process of de-industrialization, but it is certainly true that government subsidies and protections are playing an increasingly important role in keeping broadcasting alive and well. The impact of government involvement through subsidy is thus far more apparent in radio, the older of the two broadcasting media, and there is no guarantee that broadcast TV will mature in precisely the same way. The trend, however, suggests a pattern.

If, as we have argued, broadcasting was an oligopolistic industry, it should come as no surprise that the first real threat to it grew out of new market freedoms. During the Reagan administration,[9] the FCC began gradually releasing commercial broadcasters from what had, for sixty years, been their obligation to air a modicum of programming "in the public interest." For a half-century, fulfilling (or seeming to fulfill or paying lip-service to fulfilling) this vague responsibility had acted as a *quid pro quo* for whatever else broadcasters might do to maximize their profits. The consequences of the disappearance of public interest obligations in broadcasting first became apparent in the area of radio news, which many stations simply dropped from their schedules in the 1980s. Perhaps worse, the commercial licensees who kept news programming on their schedules, or even featured it, for the most part abandoned the form of vital journalism that previous generations of broadcasters had developed for the medium.

"All-news" radio stations, such as those operated by Viacom's Infinity Broadcasting division over the old AM stations founded by CBS and Westinghouse during the broadcasting era, have become little more than news/weather/traffic/headline loops, rarely devoting more than thirty seconds to a story and even less frequently editorializing or presenting anybody's viewpoint on anything beyond the prudence of installing traffic signals at busy street corners frequented by young children on their way to school. In times of national emergency, they typically cease generating anything but commercials and pick up the audio of network or cable TV coverage.

Radio journalism, like a train running daily from Chicago to New Orleans in the twenty-first century (and, as of this writing, there still is one), is now more loved by connoisseurs – people with a taste for older and subtler pleasures – than it is used by people as a practical, commercially feasible system. Just as government must subsidize that train with appropriations for Amtrak, government must provide crucial funding through the Corporation for Public Broadcasting to National Public Radio (NPR) if anything like the art of electronic journalism is to remain part of the national communication mix.[10] Even Frank Stanton, the retired CBS president who did as much as any industry executive to build the substance and reputation of commercial electronic journalism, and who was willing to go to jail to defend it (see chapter 7), admitted during a 1999 interview that NPR had, in effect, trumped his beloved CBS News since deregulation as "the best news on the air."[11]

NPR's listenership, which includes much of the American intelligentsia (and not many others), would be a lot less satisfied with the market freedoms now being exercised by the American communications industry if it did not get its broadcast news from this single, subsidized source. Though it is estimated that fewer than one in ten public radio listeners send in contributions to their local public radio stations (and that listener contributions typically constitute more than half of a public station's budget), NPR's advocates defend their tax-supported radio service with the same zeal as middle-class retirees and rail buffs who will not suffer the loss of a beloved train that is forced to travel at 35 miles per hour by the poor condition of the tracks.

Imagine how much flack Infinity would have taken for the dumbing down of CBS News (which was once, it can be said, the Pennsylvania Railroad of broadcast journalism) if NPR had not been there to mollify the intellectual needs of Volvo owners who demand the right to listen to Sylvia Poggiole explaining the plight of Albanian gypsies while making their way through traffic to get their kids to the soccer fields.

If NPR had been sold off to private interests, as Republicans proposed when they took control of the House of Representatives in 1994 for the first time since the early 1950s, American commercial radio news operations would have looked as pathetic as they actually are. There may have even been calls for the restoration of serious public interest obligations for commercial broadcasters, or licenses might have even been contested. But NPR was not privatized, even as prisons and child welfare were in some places. As conservatives from David Stockman to Newt Gingrich have learned, it is easier to cut food stamp aid to mothers of dependent children than it is to get rid of NPR or PBS[12] (or, for that matter, Amtrak). They are simply too valuable to the commercial interests that publicly ridicule them.

To be sure, Newt Gingrich, when he was newly elected as Speaker of the House, and other true-believer conservatives were ready to pounce on NPR and PBS (and, happily for our analogy, Amtrak) all at once. If NPR was saved by the way its news operation was so ably filling the vacuum left in the upmarket news niche by the descending IQ demographics of the commercial broadcasting divisions of the multi-media conglomerates, PBS was saved from privatization in large part by its children's programming. *Sesame Street*, *Mister Rogers' Neighborhood*, and other PBS kids' shows that are above suspicion for the destruction of the teeth and/or personal virtue of America's middle-class-and-up youth, had filled a vacuum equal in upmarket emptiness to the news and current affairs vacuum that NPR has filled in radio.[13] Peggy Charren, the founder of the public advocacy group Action for Children's Television, saw the failure of the privatization attempt as proof that "children's programming keeps PBS alive."[14]

That said, it is not surprising that news and business news programs are the only daily TV shows aimed at adult audiences that are carried by the PBS network. The network's flagship is *The News Hour with Jim Lehrer*. It began in 1969 as the *MacNeil–Lehrer Report*, and is a curious legacy from an era in broadcasting history when the network evening news, as presented by the likes of Walter Cronkite, John Chancellor, and Howard K. Smith, was considered too low-IQ and too brief in the attention-span department for the many people who were still thought to read newspapers. In the intervening decades, network news (circa Dan Rather, Tom Brokaw, and Peter Jennings[15]) got much dumber than anyone could have imagined forty years ago. The importance of the subsidized news on TV can be measured accordingly. Same said for PBS's *Nightly Business Report*, as compared to the market prognosticators who emerged on cable-TV financial advice programs during the dot.com boom (some of whom are under indictment or doing time).

It is not surprising that, as the aging practitioners of "old-school" electronic journalism retire or otherwise leave commercial broadcasting, they are sought as mentors not by the companies they served, but by the public broadcasting entities that are the last American practitioners of the journalism they created. Walter Cronkite, whose CBS retirement package called for him to do consulting work and produce documentaries for the network, has most notably produced and narrated science programs for PBS. Though he was heard on the CBS radio network daily for more than twenty-five years, his post-retirement radio work consists of pieces he contributes to NPR's *All Things Considered*. Reuven Frank, who headed NBC News for many years, brought the network into television dominance in the late 1950s by teaming Chet Huntley and David Brinkley in the first daily dinnertime network news program and won every award for his efforts. His post-retirement work has been as a commentator for Public Radio International's daily business-oriented news program, *Marketplace*, even though his old employer operates CNBC, a cable channel whose daytime schedule is dedicated to business news.

DAVID HARTMAN

David Hartman left conventional prime-time drama to become host of ABC's *Good Morning America* from 1976 to 1985.

DAVID HARTMAN. I talked to a friend not long ago who talked with a news director from a local station in one of America's biggest cities. A fellow tried to get a job there who was late forties, exquisite credentials as a writer, correspondent, anchor – as good as it gets. The news director said to him, "You are exactly the person whom we don't want. We want someone young, inexperienced, good-looking, charming, who will not ask questions about the ethics or quality of the stories. Go out, cover it, do the stand-up, and bring it back." Scary!

DAVID MARC. The journalistic equivalent of a "bimbo?"

DH. Correct. Scary.

David Hartman was interviewed by David Marc, New York City, October 15, 1998. Videotape and transcription, Steven H. Scheuer Collection in Television History, Center for the Study of Popular Television, Syracuse University Library. Copyright, Syracuse University 1999. An earlier interview, recorded on audiotape and transcribed, was conducted by Morton Silverstein, and is also part of the Scheuer Collection.

Robert Trout invented several of the generic reporting forms that remain in common use today, including such basics as the man-in-the-street interview and political convention floor reporting.[16] In an interview shortly before his death, he described the inglorious end to a forty-year career at CBS during which he had anchored coverage of Franklin Roosevelt's fireside chats, announced the Japanese surrender that ended the Second World War, and covered early NASA space shots. "Finally, I was getting paid just for the pieces I did and they would accept only very few. Then I was [told I was] to get $25 for a piece . . . and I just couldn't do that."[17] In 1995, at the age of 86, he was brought out of retirement by National Public Radio to do a series of features on radio coverage of the Second World War to mark the fiftieth anniversary of the end of the war.

Daniel Schorr, whose investigative work on the Watergate scandals got him fired from CBS back in the 1970s, joined NPR soon after he was let go. Three decades later, and well past the age when most commercial broadcasting journalists are kicked out of the building (or, as in Robert Trout's case, worse), he is one of

ROBERT TROUT

Robert Trout, for most of the twentieth century, was considered among the most erudite, sophisticated and well-spoken of American broadcast journalists. He interviewed presidents and kings, covered political conventions and disasters, and had the distinction of being the voice that announced to America, over the CBS radio network, that the Second World War had ended. His television career included stints on CBS, NBC, and ABC, and he returned to radio toward the end of his life as a special correspondent for NPR. Amazingly, Trout never attended college or even worked for a newspaper. Here he explains how he launched – or was launched into – a career that would make him a pioneer of radio and television journalism.

"In 1931 I was working at a radio station, WJSV [in Alexandria Virginia] writing as an unpaid volunteer worker. A reporter would come over to the station every day from the *Alexandria Gazette* to do an evening broadcast, which meant reading from the newspaper. *That* was our news broadcast. It was free, of course, but it advertised the *Gazette*. Well, the man didn't appear one day. As the time approached to begin the broadcast, somebody sat me in a chair, pushed a microphone in my face, and gave me a copy of that day's *Gazette*. I didn't know what I was doing, but I just sat there and read the paper into the microphone. The manager, who heard the broadcast while he was at dinner, came back and said, 'That new guy who came over is better than the other one. Let's get him. Who was it?' I was absolutely astounded, because I'd always been in the habit of mumbling and never speaking up, at least according to my elders. Even now, a waiter will ask me three times what I just ordered. But it turned out, I suppose, that under a microphone I must have sounded differently."

Robert Trout was interviewed by Steven H. Scheuer, New York City, October 12, 1998. Videotape and transcription, Steven H. Scheuer Collection in Television History, Center for the Study of Popular Television, Syracuse University Library. Copyright Syracuse University 1999. An earlier interview, recorded on audiotape and transcribed, was conducted by Ron Simon and is also part of the Scheuer Collection.

a very few senior reporters who delivers news analysis on the radio. The commercial competition consists of Paul Harvey.

The Shock of the News

It would be easy to ennoble the Age of Broadcasting as a golden time when tens of millions of Americans, hungering for a knowledge of current events in their home towns, the nation, and the world, pressed their ears to the radio and, later, their noses to the TV set, for daily news reports, presidential press conferences, coverage of international conflicts, and so on. The truth, as is so often the case, is something less grand. Subsequent history seems to indicate that the chief reason for the large pre-cable news audience was that most of the time when news was being broadcast, there was nothing else on. This was due to two factors, which we examined earlier, which are rapidly fading into the obscure subject known as broadcasting history: (1) channels were scarce then because of the limitations of the over-the-air spectrum; and (2) FCC licensing standards, then still in existence, were easily met by all the competitors in a given broadcasting market by counterprogramming news shows against each other, with a few public affairs series at 4 a.m. or so thrown in for good measure. Cable TV and video appliances ended the scarcity problem, and a pop revival of get-the-government-off-of-our-backs capitalism took care of the rest of it.[18]

Offered an increasing number of alternatives, increasing chunks of the mass audience soon demonstrated the same indifference toward broadcast news that they had been showing toward newspapers since the advent of broadcasting. Commercial radio news shriveled into headline scraps and traffic jam sightings aimed at the millions of Americans who spend their days riding around metropolitan freeway systems practicing one form or another of service-economy commerce. At the same time, TV news was boutiquing into a taste culture item for "news junkies" who, with remote in one hand and mouse in the other, surf the news sources during their spare time – even when there isn't an actual war in progress.

To a mind formed during the Age of Broadcasting, it might follow logically that less broadcast news would have been accompanied by more, and perhaps even better, prime-time dramatic programming on the broadcast networks. However, other conditions of the post-cable entertainment order prevented this from happening. With broadcast network audience share dwindling, but prime-time production costs – especially for stars – not, the over-the-air networks found themselves looking for low-overhead programming ideas, especially formats that would avoid the ever-growing burden of star salaries. Two genres met this need and proliferated through turn-of-Century-21 television: news magazines, which grew in number and frequency; and reality TV shows, which grew in number and freakishness.

SYLVESTER "PAT" WEAVER

Pat Weaver was an advertising executive with Young & Rubicam during the radio age and he became the first president of NBC Television in 1947. Here he recalls some of the difficulties he had in getting highly educated sponsors to take a dispassionate attitude toward "low-brow" entertainers.

"I remember, to my astonishment and horror, when I went to Mr. Little, the head of Colgate, to try to get him to buy Jackie Gleason, who had been a guest on *The Colgate Comedy Hour*, for the permanent hosting job on the show. Mr. Little's comment was, 'I don't want that fat slob on my show again.' Another time, I was going over a list of 'possibles' with him and he said, 'Who is this fellow Abbott N. Costello that you're talking about?'"

Sylvester "Pat" Weaver was interviewed by Steven H. Scheuer, Los Angeles, in the spring of 1996. Videotape and transcription, Steven H. Scheuer Collection in Television History, Center for the Study of Popular Television, Syracuse University Library. Copyright Syracuse University 1999.

In the case of the former, the heritage networks (ABC, CBS, NBC) were attracted by the opportunity to use the fixed costs of their news divisions – including the salaries of correspondents, writers and other production personnel – to generate what amounted to bargain material for prime-time entertainment. The magazine idea itself was nothing new. Pat Weaver, the first head of NBC television, foresaw it in the early 1950s as a mold from which the entire television day might be cast. The original designs of such Weaver programming creations as the *Today Show* (early morning), *Home* (midday), and the *Tonight Show* were essentially magazines, with their emphases shifting to suit the rhythms of the day.[19] After Weaver left NBC, however, the magazine synthesis all but disappeared from the two surviving series, with *Tonight* dropping its news component to become an entertainment vehicle (it had once contained a daily wrap-up from a news correspondent) and *Today* becoming a news division production (it had once featured the chimpanzee J. Fredd Muggs as a cast regular).

The most immediate model for the contemporary news magazine is CBS's *60 Minutes*, which premiered in 1968 (see chapter 6). CBS television, which had a tradition of presenting prime-time news division productions, including such honored series as *See It Now*, *The Twentieth Century*, and *CBS Reports*, had gradually pulled all weekly news and documentary programs from its prime-time schedule during the early 1960s, giving the slots to more profitable entertainment series. However, seeing a practical need to display the public face of its news division during the most-watched hours (and to quell the resentment of its star reporters) the network settled upon a format. Like the general-interest print magazine (a form that, ironically, was killed by television), *60 Minutes* was designed to offer a range of stories, including information on current events, interviews with movie stars, and even an occasional muckraking piece. Despite low ratings during its early years, *60 Minutes* had the unusual advantage of being carried by a network that was determined to tweak it into success. The show eventually made its way to the Top Ten after being rescheduled into the early Sunday evening period, after NFL football.

In 1978, as ABC was succeeding in its thirty-year struggle for ratings parity with CBS and NBC, the network introduced *20/20*, a *60 Minutes* knock-off fashioned by its recently hired news division chief, Roone Arledge, the first executive with no formal training or experience as a journalist to head a network news division. As chief of ABC Sports, Arledge had created such successes as *ABC's Monday Night Football* and *ABC's Wide World of Sports*, and was known as a proponent of what is, today, called "branding" in mass communications.[20]

Arledge saw a prime-time window as an important branding tool for ABC News, whose correspondents generally lacked the recognition and viewer loyalty that CBS had created for its news stars by giving them a regular platform in prime time. As was the case with *60 Minutes*, *20/20* was a ratings disaster in its early years; however, in true faith to the model, Arledge kept the show on the schedule until he found a successful commercial formula for it. This occurred in 1984, the series' sixth season, when he recast the hosting spot by teaming gushing celebrity interviewer Barbara Walters as co-host with the avuncular Hugh Downs, a dignified former game show host whose résumé included sidekick on the *Tonight Show* under the regime of host Jack Paar.

Throughout the 1980s, NBC tried repeatedly to create a prime-time magazine to give the same kind of promotional boost to its news personalities as its two rivals were getting from *60 Minutes* and *20/20*. The network, however, showed little of the patience that its rivals had demonstrated. Quick cancellations created a collection of failures that soon became the stuff of stand-up comedy routines, including barbs from Johnny Carson in his daily *Tonight Show* monologues on NBC.

The network finally found a news magazine signature in 1992 with the premiere of *Dateline*. The show's success can be at least partially attributed to the publicity created during its first year when it was revealed that *Dateline* producers had staged, for the cameras, a phony test-crash explosion of a General Motors pick-up truck in an "exposé" of the vehicle's defective gas tank. As had been the case in the 1950s when quiz shows, including NBC's *Twenty-One*, had been rigged to insure viewer

MARLENE SANDERS

Marlene Sanders, during a long career in television news and public affairs at ABC, CBS, and PBS, won three Emmy awards and broke many barriers for women in television journalism. In 1964, for example, she became the first woman to anchor a prime-time network news broadcast, when she substituted for ABC anchor Ron Cochran, who had laryngitis. In 1976, while a producer-correspondent for ABC's documentary unit, she became the first woman vice-president at a network news division. Here she talks about the difficulties she faced at ABC News during the late 1970s.

"We discovered in our women's groups that the sports department was one of the major villains at ABC. Sexual harassment wasn't a word used then, but the women who worked in sports were constantly subjected to the casting couch and the kind of language in the control room at sports events, you know, 'Get the boob shot' – all that kind of thing. It was notorious and complaints . . . were basically ignored. So when Roone Arledge [head of ABC Sports] was made president of news, I thought, 'Oh, God, this is terrible.' I had very little contact with him. I never really got to know him. I was head of a department, but he practically would never meet with me or answer my calls. I went about my business, but I was working in a vacuum. [My work] was good, but I had to start thinking about my next job. I had been at ABC nearly 14 years at that point and was in my late 40s. I was getting a little old to be a correspondent, at least from what I could see and who was out there. . . . I had no support from the men who were the other vice presidents."

In 1978 Sanders joined CBS News.

Marlene Sanders was interviewed by Morton Silverstein, New York City, November 8, 1996. Audiotape and transcription, Steven H. Scheuer Collection in Television History, Center for the Study of Popular Television, Syracuse University Library. Copyright Syracuse University 1999. The picture of Sanders is from a later interview, videotaped and transcribed, which was conducted by Les Brown and is also part of the Scheuer Collection.

interest, there can be little doubt that an exploding truck was, indeed, a superior entertainment product in comparison to a non-exploding truck. It can even be argued that, knowing the vehicle to be dangerous (based on the evidence of actual past explosions), the producers were merely putting art in the service of public safety. In any case, critics were outraged that viewers had not been informed by NBC of the difference between art and The News. There wasn't even one of those minuscule, unreadable disclaimers that they sometimes use on these kinds of programs when they're showing animated graphics of a story that would have otherwise had no footage.

The dual consequences of the exploding *Dateline* truck scandal mark a cusp moment in the historical development of broadcast news: (1) in a homage to the best traditions of American journalism (from, let's say, Peter Zenger to Walter Cronkite), the head of NBC News was forced to resign by the network's high-minded top brass; and (2) *Dateline* had earned for itself a permanent spot on the NBC prime-time schedule from the network's high-ratings-minded top brass.

Accordingly, the 1990s marked a period of unprecedented decay in broadcast journalism. Whereas two decades earlier, facing the threat of jail, Frank Stanton had withheld video outtakes and names of sources used in a CBS documentary concerning corruption at the Pentagon, the CBS of the 1990s was cowed by the tobacco industry into suppressing a piece concerning what and when industry executives knew about the ill effects of smoking.

The networks, as always, set the standards for their o&os and affiliates. Beyond that, they greased the slippery slope with pointed suggestions for news stories that were little more than promotions for upcoming network entertainment shows. Local stations around the country, relieved of the crushing burden of public service obligations to cover local issues, which had gained them their broadcasting licenses, seemed happy to take network advice to do stories on forms of cancer or mental illness and schedule them in conjunction with made-for-television movies that use them as storylines.

The FOX network, which offered no national daily news broadcast at all, played its special part in redefining standards by presenting the autopsy of an extraterrestial in prime time. Elsewhere on the dial, Geraldo Rivera took viewers on a historical journey to the secret hiding place of Al Capone's buried treasure – NOT. "I could have rigged the thing by checking it out first, and filling it up with jewelry and spectacular valuables," Rivera told the meta-press, "but I chose *not to* because I'm a journalist and have the public trust. Yet did anyone think to consider me for a DuPont Award, or a Peabody, or even a Christopher, for the way I handled the whole thing? Not that I know about."[21] A lot could be done in the name of The News now that news no longer occupied the special status of a legal obligation demanding qualitative measurement by pre-existing standards. The News itself was becoming an imitation of the news magazine, which had begun by mimicking it.

Many broadcast journalists were unhappy with what looked like a debasement of the public credibility that their news divisions had struggled to build since the radio era. A few critics were even willing to discuss the larger threat contained in a fast and loose willingness to sensationalize mediocre fictions by invoking the sacred mantle of The Press (as in *"freedom* of the press") to gain unearned credibility and secure constitutionally guaranteed immunity from the consequences of their charades.

Joan Konner, publisher of the *Columbia Journalism Review* and Dean Emerita of the Columbia Journalism School, was among them. Asked about the decline of television journalism during the cable age in a 1998 interview, she said,

> I keep holding on to the idealistic belief that somebody is going to break out of the pack as the [news] audience splinters; that somebody will emerge because of a commitment to quality and a commitment to a broader agenda. But the entire definition of news is now open to challenge. I'm not talking about the hard political news, of which the news organizations see themselves as a watchdog of power. That will always be a prime need in a democratic society. But . . . people want to learn more. The reason why people listen to NPR is because it does teach them more, on a wider variety of subjects. There needs to be a breakaway from what I call "the journalism of fear"; that is, news based on what you have to be afraid of, with the abuse of power being one of those things and bad weather being another.[22]

The free-fall of broadcast news standards in prime time was finally offered a plateau – a position from which it could define and defend itself – by the increasing popularity of reality TV. Anything too ridiculous to be called journalism could be classified as a "reality" show rather than "news," with production responsibility kicked cleanly to the lower expectations of the entertainment division. Entertainment producers, for their part, were happy with the arrangement, which freed them, simultaneously, from the two things they liked least: (1) the "credibility thing," which constrained news magazines from following their entertainment instincts; and (2) the salaries of star actors. In fact, reality shows presented opportunities to work without using any professional actors at all, as most performers in a reality vehicle ask nothing more for their services than a chance to appear on national television. As if that overhead saving is not godsend enough, you can even have some of your nastiest production costs – car crashes, burning buildings, ambulances racing through the streets – picked up by taxpayer-supported municipal agencies.

The Third Mask of Janus

Though reality programming is usually referred to as a "genre" of television (a convenience we took advantage of earlier), it is developing in a way that indicates it may be something more than a mere program type. Reality TV (RTV) is perhaps better understood as a revolutionary (and we don't use that term often), media-age equal partner to those two long-running Aristotelian mega-genres, comedy and tragedy. At its best, RTV is full of comic elements, especially humor and confusion, as well as the kind of challenges to moral sensibility that are associated with tragic drama. However, reality shows depart from traditional dramatic art in that they do not depend on either catharsis (tragedy) or the restoration of harmony (comedy) for satisfactory conclusions. Instead, they are more likely to invoke existential reality as, of all things, a *deus ex machina* that rescues them from violating their scheduled time slot.

Unscripted filming using a hidden camera, the rawest and therefore the purest voyeuristic form of RTV, offers us the employee urinating into the coffee pot in the back room of the workplace, as in *Busted on the Job*. At its most theatrical – scripted filming with a hidden camera – RTV offers us a person having a two-way conversation with a house plant, as in *Candid Camera*, a show created by reality TV pioneer Allen Funt, who began developing the form on radio during the 1940s with his *Candid Microphone* series.

The most successful reality series in prime time usually synthesize elements of *ciné-vérité* (or cinema *vérité*), which was conceived of for use in muckraking documentaries, with familiar elements of dramatic genres. In *Cops*, the longest-running of the original FOX television network shows, *vérité* meets the old-fashioned TV cop show, à la *Adam-12* or *Starsky and Hutch*. Combining elements of these dramas with documentary realism, a typical *Cops* episode is likely to yield, in the editing room, a catch from its own familiar pool of archetypal perps: shirtless drunken rednecks, defiant drunk drivers, African American teenage boys up to no good, and so on.

In MTV's *The Real World*, street crime is traded for puberty and related identity crises as the "reality" catalysts. *Vérité* conjugates with soap opera and, again, recognizable characters are key. Studboy, virgin, slutgirl, gay guy, bohemian, and others mix it up emotionally in an overstudied search for self. Public casting calls – no résumés required, no union cards allowed – draw thousands seeking nothing more than an unpaid internship in celebrity. How does a non-actor prepare? By watching RTV and trying on the personality costume that best fits.

In *Tough Enough*, another MTV series, Holden Caulfield meets Hulk Hogan, putting mimetic theory to an even more severe test. Wannabees are not only challenged to prove their ability to transform their personality into an artistic persona, but they must also harness their athletic skills in the service of choreography. The prize? A ticket out of mass culture palookaville via a contract with World Wrestling Entertainment, where anybody can be a contender. ABC's *Are You Hot?*, in which people strip down to show all but genitalia to be "rated" for their degree of physical perfection, uses a storyline previously restricted to pornography videos.

It may well mark the last leg of a psychosexual journey in American mass culture that began with the imposition of the Hays Code on Hollywood films in the 1930s.[23]

The starkest reality presented by reality television at its best is a demystification of the medium of television. TV began penetrating American life when crowds first gathered in front of appliance stores to stand and behold the miracle of Milton Berle. Despite its placement in the home, television maintained the olympian aura of the theater (via cinema), a place where only gods, goddesses, and the extreme cases of humanity could appear. Those days, of course, are gone. Children put tapes into VCRs and fast-forward them when bored, which is often soon, and eject them in favor of others when they lose interest completely. Parents begin taping their children at the birth moment and keep video tabs of first steps, birthday parties, and everything else until the children's emerging sexual personalities force them to abandon camera. Once they have become too dangerous to appear in parent productions, the children make their own tapes. As in most human endeavors, those who see themselves as extraordinary in some way – in appearance, in performance, in charisma, or in the effective practice of good and/or evil – are ready to move on to the next level. Reality is waiting: *The Bachelor, Road Rules, Survivor, Who Wants to be a Millionaire?, MTV Spring Break Coverage, The Jerry Springer Show.*

The Summer of Reality began in May 2000, with the premiere of *Survivor*. The success of the CBS prime-time series marked the emergence of reality as a fully fledged network programming phenomenon, worthy of cookie-cutter imitations, late-night spoofs, and public obsession. By its final episode, some 62 million viewers had seen one or more episodes and the *"Survivor* phenomenon" had saturated mass cultural conversation like a number 1 hit from the 1960s. Broadcast network television had found what it needed: an inexpensive programming form that promised to put it, if only occasionally now, squarely at the center of conversation at the office water cooler, above, beyond, and beneath demographic lines. Imitations followed: *Big Brother, Temptation Island, Fear Factor, The Amazing Race,* and so on. Many people who watch television are already bored.

Notes

1   Pat Robertson, interviewed by David Marc, Virginia Beach, Virginia, February 16, 2000. Videotape and transcription, oral history collections, Center for the Study of Popular Television, Syracuse University Library. Copyright Syracuse University 2000. The interview was made possible by a grant from the Lilly Endowment Inc.

2   Frank Stanton, interviewed by David Marc, New York City, May 21, 1999. Audiotape and transcription, Steven H. Scheuer Collection in Television History, Center for the Study of Popular Television, Syracuse University Library. Copyright Syracuse University, 1999.

3   The anti-social security plank would remain in the Republican Party platform until 1968 when Richard Nixon, ever the pragmatist/opportunist, demanded its removal.

4   Senator Trent Lott of Mississippi was forced to resign his position as Republican majority leader in the Senate in 2002 when expressing support for Thurmond's 1948 campaign. In the past, while rising to the position of Republican leader, he had made similar statements in public, and had even expressed support for a white supremacist organization, where he appeared as a guest speaker. Why all the fuss this time? He had made his statements on television (C-SPAN). Perhaps his nostalgia for 1948 had erased the power of television itself from his mind.

5   For further reading on this subject see the poem by Wallace Stevens, "The Idea of Order at Key West" (1951), in *Collected Poetry and Prose Wallace Stevens* (New York: Library of America, 1997).

6   "A Survey of Television," *The Economist*, April 13, 2002, p. 3.

7   Ibid.

8   These government subsidies were "highly visible" as compared to the technologies that passenger trains had to compete with: cheaper car and bus travel made possible by the invisible subsidies of government road-building and maintenance; and faster air travel, invisibly subsidized by government air-traffic control systems and airport building and maintenance.

9   Ronald Reagan served two four-year terms as President of the United States from 1980 to 1988.

10   By "the art of electronic journalism," we refer to the methods of audio reporting created by Edward R. Murrow, Robert Trout, Howard K. Smith, and others, which were adapted by their practitioners for early television broadcasting.

11   Frank Stanton, interviewed by David Marc, May 21, 1999 (see note 2 above).

12   PBS: Public Broadcasting System.

13   While relatively safe from charges of dental menace, *Sesame Street*, *The Electric Company*, and other PBS children's programs produced by the Children's Television Workshop have been criticized for capitulating on length of attention-span. See Neil Postman, *Amusing Ourselves To Death* (New York: Viking, 1985).

14   Peggy Charren, interviewed by David Marc, Boston, May 5, 1999. Audiotape and transcription, Steven H. Scheuer Collection in Television History, Center for the Study of Popular Television, Syracuse University Library. Copyright Syracuse University, 1999.

15   No criticism of the journalistic abilities of Rather, Brokaw, or Jennings is meant. The communications business changed and they stayed for the money. The same can be said of just about every successful American newspaper, magazine, and book editor born before 1950.

16   For a sketch of Robert Trout's remarkable career see David Marc's biographical article on Trout in *Oxford's American National Biography Online, www.anb.com*.

17   Robert Trout interviewed by Ron Simon at Mr. Trout's home in New York City, March 2, 1998. Audiotape and transcription, Steven H. Scheuer Collection in Television History, Center for the Study of Popular Television, Syracuse University Library. Copyright Syracuse University, 1999. It is only fair to mention that, after severing his

relationship with CBS, he did join ABC News for a time. "They were a young group and needed a grand old man," he said.

18 The pronoun "our" in the phrase "get the government off of *our* backs" refers here to the several dozen multi-million-dollar corporations that own television and radio stations.

19 See Pat Weaver, *Best Seat in the House* (New York: Knopf, 1994). In his autobiography, Weaver elaborates on these programming ideas.

20 "Branding," in contemporary mass communications, refers to the practice of creating a public identity for a particular product that makes it synonymous with the generic product and thus indicates dependability and quality. Early examples include Kleenex, a brand of tissues; Jello, a brand of gelatin; and Frigidaire, a brand of refrigerator. In the UK, Hoover vacuum cleaners have achieved this status, though the Hoover brand has not achieved this status in the US.

21 Rivera did not actually say this. We wrote the quotation ourselves and inserted it to make two important points: (1) the ease with which people can be misled by the implied authority of a medium (whether it is a television program or a book); and (2) the importance of reading footnotes and other documentation. It's not just busy work!

22 Joan Konner, interviewed by David Marc, New York City, December 21, 1998. Audiotape and transcription, Steven H. Scheuer Collection in Television History, Center for the Study of Popular Television, Syracuse University Library. Copyright Syracuse University 1999.

23 In 1930, the National Board of Review, a body controlled by the major film studios and headed by Judge Will H. Hays of Indiana, issued a set of guidelines concerning what could and could not be shown in film. Officially known as the Production Code, it was more commonly referred to as the "Hays Code." Joseph Breen, a Hays appointee, was in charge of the Production Code administration. Films were reviewed for their adherence to the code before they could be put into the mass distribution system. For example, a murderer had to die or wind up behind bars at the conclusion of a film; if a man and a woman were in a bedroom, three of their four feet had to be on the ground. See Raymond Moley, *The Hays Office* (Indianapolis: Bobbs-Merrill, 1945) for an exhaustive study, including a printing of the code. See Robert Sklar's *Movie Made America* (New York: Vintage, 1994) for a discussion in historical context of the Hays Code and the American film industry's system of self-censorship during most of the twentieth century.

INDEX